The Second World War
A Captivating Guide to World War II and D Day

Contents

FREE BONUS FROM CAPTIVATING HISTORY (AVAILABLE FOR A LIMITED TIME)..9

PART 1: WORLD WAR 2..1
A CAPTIVATING GUIDE FROM BEGINNING TO END 1

INTRODUCTION..2

CHAPTER 1 – THE RISING TIDE..3

CHAPTER 2 – FROM POLAND TO THE FALL OF FRANCE..........7

CHAPTER 3 – BRITAIN'S DARKEST HOUR 13

CHAPTER 4 – BARBAROSSA UNLEASHED..............................18

CHAPTER 5 – EARLY OPERATIONS IN AFRICA AND THE MEDITERRANEAN 24

CHAPTER 6 – A DAY WHICH WILL LIVE IN INFAMY.............29

CHAPTER 7 – GERMANY'S EASTERN OFFENSIVES 34

CHAPTER 8 – GUADALCANAL AND THE WAR IN ASIA 40

CHAPTER 9 – OPERATION TORCH AND THE TAKING OF NORTH AFRICA 46

CHAPTER 10 – THE TIDE TURNS IN EASTERN EUROPE 52

CHAPTER 11 – ADVANCING ON JAPAN 58

CHAPTER 12 – THE INVASION OF ITALY 64

CHAPTER 13 – FROM D-DAY TO THE BULGE 70

CHAPTER 14 – THE FALL OF GERMANY 77

CHAPTER 15 – THE FALL OF JAPAN 83

CHAPTER 16 – AFTERMATH 88

CONCLUSION 91

Part 2: D Day 92

A Captivating Guide to the Battle for Normandy 92

INTRODUCTION 93

CHAPTER 1 – WHY D-DAY? 94

CHAPTER 2 – PREPARATION 99

CHAPTER 3 – DECEPTION 107

CHAPTER 4 – THE COMMANDERS 112

CHAPTER 5 – THE MEN AND EQUIPMENT 120

CHAPTER 6 – THE GERMAN DEFENSES 125

CHAPTER 7 – THE PARATROOPER LANDINGS 131

CHAPTER 8 – OMAHA..136

CHAPTER 9 – UTAH...143

CHAPTER 10 – GOLD..148

CHAPTER 11 – JUNO..153

CHAPTER 12 – SWORD..158

CHAPTER 13 – THE RESISTANCE..164

CHAPTER 14 –ADVANCE...168

CHAPTER 15 – BREAKOUT...174

CONCLUSION...180

PREVIEW OF ADOLF HITLER...183

INTRODUCTION...183

PART I — ORIGINS..187

THE SON OF ALOIS AND KLARA..187
PREVIEW OF WINSTON CHURCHILL:...193

INTRODUCTION...193

CHAPTER ONE: CHURCHILL'S PERSONAL LIFE....................196

CONTINUE READING!...203

PREVIEW OF FRANKLIN ROOSEVELT:..204

INTRODUCTION...204

CHAPTER ONE: CHILDHOOD AND EDUCATION....................207

CONTINUE READING!...214

FREE BONUS FROM CAPTIVATING HISTORY (AVAILABLE FOR A LIMITED TIME) 216

BIBLIOGRAPHY 217

Free Bonus from Captivating History (Available for a Limited time)

Hi History Lovers!

Now you have a chance to join our exclusive history list so you can get your first history ebook for free as well as discounts and a potential to get more history books for free! Simply visit the link below to join.

Captivatinghistory.com/ebook

Also, make sure to follow us on:

Twitter: @Captivhistory

Facebook: Captivating History: @captivatinghistory

Part 1: World War 2
A Captivating Guide from Beginning to End

Introduction

The Second World War was one of the most traumatic events in human history. Across the world, existing conflicts became connected, entangling nations in a vast web of violence. It was fought on land, sea, and air, touching every inhabited continent. Over 55 million people died, some of them combatants, some civilians caught up in the violence, and some murdered by their own governments.

It was the war that unleashed the Holocaust and the atomic bomb upon the world. But it was also a war that featured acts of courage and self-sacrifice on every side.

The world would never be the same again.

Chapter 1 – The Rising Tide

The Second World War grew out of conflicts in two parts of the world: Europe and East Asia. Though the two would eventually become entangled, it's easier to understand the causes of the war by looking at them separately.

Europe's problems were rooted in centuries of competition between powerful nations crammed together on a small and densely populated continent. Most of the world's toughest, most stubborn, and most ambitious kids were crammed together in a single small playground. Conflict was all but inevitable.

The most recent large European conflict had been the First World War. This was the first industrialized war, a hugely traumatic event for all the participants. In the aftermath, Germany was severely punished for its aggression by the victorious Allied powers. The remains of the Austro-Hungarian empire fell apart, creating instability in the east. And the Russian Empire, whose government had been overthrown during the turmoil of the war, became the Union of Soviet Socialist Republics (USSR), the first global power to adopt the new ideology of communism.

From this situation of instability, a new form of politics emerged. Across Europe, extreme right-wing parties adopted ultra-nationalistic views. Many of them incorporated ideas of racial superiority. Most were strongly influenced by the fear of communism. All relied on scapegoating outsiders to make themselves more powerful.

The first to reach prominence was the Fascist Party in Italy under Benito Mussolini. Mussolini was a veteran soldier, gifted orator, and skilled administrator. He rallied disenchanted left-wingers and those who felt put down by corrupt politicians and forceful trade unions. Using a mixture of persuasion and intimidation, he won the 1922 election and became prime minister. Through a series of laws, he turned his country into a one-party dictatorship. Most of his achievements were domestic, bringing order and efficiency at the price of freedom, but he also had ambitions abroad. He wanted Italy to be a colonial power like Britain or France, and so in 1935-6 his forces conquered Abyssinia.

Mussolini was surpassed in almost every way by the man who reached power in Germany a decade later—Adolph Hitler. A decorated veteran of the First World War, Hitler was embittered at the Versailles Treaty, which imposed crushing restrictions upon Germany in the aftermath of the war. He developed a monstrous ideology that combined racism, homophobia, and a bitter hatred of communism. Like Mussolini, he brought together oratory and street violence to seize control of Germany. Once elected chancellor in 1933, he purged all opposition and had himself made Führer, the nation's "leader" or "guide." He then escalated the rearmament of Germany, casting off the shackles of Versailles.

Hitler and Mussolini intervened in the Spanish Civil War of 1936-9. Rather than have their nations join the war, they sent parts of their armed forces to support Franco's right-wing armies, testing new military technology and tactics while ensuring the victory of a man they expected to be an ally—a man who would in fact keep his nation out of the coming war for Europe.

Meanwhile, Hitler was playing a game of chicken with the other European powers. In March 1936, he occupied the Rhineland, a part of Germany that had been demilitarized after the war. Two years later, he annexed his own homeland of Austria, with its large German-speaking population. He occupied parts of Czechoslovakia that fall and finished the job off the following spring. At every turn, the rest of Europe backed down rather than go to war to protect less powerful nations.

Meanwhile, in Asia, the Chinese revolutions of 1911 and 1913, along with the Chinese Civil War that broke out in 1927, had triggered a parallel period of instability. Nationalists and communists battled for control of a vast nation, destroying the regional balance of power.

Japan was a nation on the rise. Economic growth had created a sense of ambition which had then been threatened by a downturn in the 1930s. Interventions by Western powers, including their colonies in Asia and a restrictive naval treaty of 1930, embittered many in Japan, who saw the Europeans and Americans as colonialist outsiders meddling in their part of the world.

The Japanese began a period of expansion, looking to increase their political dominance and their control of valuable raw resources. They invaded Chinese Manchuria in 1931 and from then on kept encroaching on Chinese territory. At last, in 1937, the Chinese nationalist leader Chiang Kai-Shek gave up on his previous policy of giving ground to buy himself time. A minor skirmish escalated into the Second Sino-Japanese War.

From an Asian point of view, the war had already begun. But it would be Hitler who pushed Europe over the brink and gave the war its Western start date of 1939.

Chapter 2 – From Poland to the Fall of France

Hitler had long looked at Poland with hungry eyes. He believed in the racial superiority of Germans and wanted more space for them to live in. Poland, just over the border to the east, was perfect. Many Nazi supporters had fought against Polish incursions following the First World War, and so they were already primed for conflict with the Poles.

On September 1, 1939, German troops swept across the Polish border. It was a war the Germans had long been preparing for. Under the secret terms of the Molotov-Ribbentrop Pact, Germany and the USSR had agreed not only to keep the peace between themselves but to partition Poland between them. Meanwhile, German forces had been gathering on the Polish border.

Fifty-five German divisions swept into Poland. These were primarily tanks and motorized infantry, allowing them to advance swiftly. The Luftwaffe, the German air force, pounded the Polish defenses. With only 17 divisions at the front and 22 more preparing, the Poles were vastly outnumbered. It was the same in the air, where 4,700 modern German planes faced the 842 outdated aircraft of the Polish air force. On top of this, some German troops were already experienced soldiers, veterans of the fighting in Spain.

This was the first example of what came to be called Blitzkrieg—"lightning war." German commanders such as Heinz Guderian had long been advocating such a fast-paced, hard-hitting form of warfare. The open plains of Poland were the perfect place to showcase what they could do.

The Germans advanced 140 miles in the first week, reaching the borders of Warsaw. There, at the Polish capital, some of the fiercest fighting took place.

On September 17, the Russians invaded Poland from the east. Most of the Polish forces had already been smashed by the Germans. The following day, the Polish high command fled into exile. Eighty thousand soldiers followed them, fleeing to France and Britain. The Warsaw garrison surrendered on September 28, the last substantial Polish forces on October 5.

The Poles had powerful allies. They had had a treaty with France since 1921 and one with Britain since 1939. On September 3, Britain and France declared war on Germany. Australia, Canada, New Zealand, and South Africa, all independent dominions within the British Commonwealth, followed their parent country's lead. But none of them were close enough to help as Poland was engulfed.

The months that followed are often referred to as the "phony war" due to the lack of direct conflict between the major belligerents. But this hides the frantic activity going on across Europe.

While the invasion of Poland was still underway, the French made a brief and half-hearted attempt to invade the German Saarland, only to run up against the carefully prepared defenses of the Siegfried Line.

In the east, the USSR began swallowing up territory not yet occupied by the Germans. This included a grueling invasion of Finland, known as the Winter War, in which poorly prepared Soviet troops became bogged down in bitter cold that stopped vehicles from working and froze men to death. Though the Russians gained territory from the Finns, it was in many ways a Pyrrhic victory.

The Allies began a naval blockade of Germany. The power of the British Royal Navy gave them a huge advantage. The Germans countered with submarines, known as U-boats, which slipped out into the Atlantic to attack convoys bringing vital war supplies to Britain and France. These supplies included equipment hastily ordered from the Americans, who were happy to play a profitable part in bolstering friendly nations without entangling themselves in a European war.

Meanwhile, Polish troops arrived in Britain and France. They brought with them cryptographers who had begun work on breaking the Enigma code, used for Germany's highest-level military communications. This fed into the work of British military intelligence, which in a matter of months was turned from a neglected corner of government into the world's leading organization for covert information gathering and analysis.

In April 1940, Germany invaded Denmark and Norway to protect shipping routes for vital iron ore from Sweden. British, French, and Polish troops rushed to support the Norwegians. But once again, the Germans swiftly overwhelmed their opponents.

One important result of the failure in Norway was a change of government in Britain. On May 10, 1940, Winston Churchill replaced Neville Chamberlain as prime minister. Churchill, long a belligerent and divisive figure in British politics, formed a coalition government that united the country for war. His strong leadership would prove vital in the days ahead.

Just as Churchill was taking up his new role, Germany was preparing for its most dramatic success of the war—the invasion of France. As forces gathered on the western border over the winter, the German army had adopted a revised plan of action developed by Field Marshal Erich von Manstein. Manstein's plan shifted the focus of the German offensive south, so that the main strike would come through the Ardennes forest, a region supposedly impassable to a modern army. That change of plan proved critical.

One hundred and thirty-six German army divisions had been gathered for the invasion. Facing them were 94 French, 22 Belgian, and 10 British divisions. The Germans had fewer tanks than their opponents, but the superior quality of those tanks and the skill of tank commanders such as Guderian and Erwin Rommel would give the Germans the advantage in armored forces.

On May 10, 1940, the Germans launched their attack.

In the Netherlands, the Dutch army was swiftly overwhelmed by the forces of their more powerful neighbor. The Dutch surrendered after only four days of fighting.

In Belgium, the attack began with the arrival of German paratroopers on the roof of the massive concrete fort at Eben Emael, part of a defensive system along the Albert Canal. The paratroopers destroyed the gun turrets and defeated a garrison that outnumbered them more than ten to one. With the Belgian defensive line weakened, its armies outnumbered, and half the air force quickly destroyed, the nation was swiftly overrun with German troops.

At the southern end of the advance, German Panzer divisions—fast-moving units consisting of tanks and their supporting troops—raced through the Ardennes in southern Belgium and burst into France. The French had not been prepared for an attack in this area and so the Germans hit them at the point where two of their weakest armies joined. The Germans quickly broke through, fought their way across the River Meuse, and then raced northwest. On May 20, they reached the English Channel, splitting the Allied forces in half.

The British Expeditionary Force, along with French and other Allied troops, were surrounded on a shrinking patch of ground. On May 26, the British began evacuating these beleaguered troops through the port of Dunkirk, while a French rearguard held off the Germans; 338,000 men, including 120,000 French, were evacuated. Their survival was vital to maintaining the Allied war effort and helped to boost morale back in Britain, but some in France saw this as a betrayal, abandoning them in their hour of need.

With the Channel coast clear, the Germans swept south, surrounding the bulk of the remaining French troops. Many of the French were stationed on the Maginot Line, a system of concrete fortresses that the Germans had simply bypassed with their Ardennes offensive. Once again, the French were outmaneuvered and overwhelmed.

The French, militarily beaten, surrendered on June 22. The country was divided. The north and west were occupied by the Germans. The southeast became a puppet state under the right-wing Vichy regime.

Meanwhile, on June 10, Mussolini sent troops across the Alps into southeastern France. It was a token effort to claim some glory and territory before Hitler got it all. More importantly, it brought Italy into the war.

Chapter 3 – Britain's Darkest Hour

The months that followed have achieved near-legendary status in Britain, and not without reason. Half of Europe had been overrun by the Axis powers of Germany and Italy. The nations that hadn't been conquered, including Sweden, Ireland, and Spain, remained neutral. Of the sovereign states of Europe, only Britain stood against an alliance of aggressive regimes.

As is so often the case, the truth is far less simple than the legend, and the British were never really alone.

In Britain, the armed forces were suddenly bolstered by a wave of refugees—soldiers, airmen, and seamen who had survived the fall of their countries and come to fight with Britain against a mutual enemy. The French brought substantial forces led by General de Gaulle. Evacuees from Poland included airmen, soldiers, and the vital specialists who had been researching the Enigma code.

Further afield, Britain was supported by the remains of its empire and by the Commonwealth, a collection of ex-imperial nations. Of the most prominent imperial and Commonwealth states, Australia and India would both contribute to the war in Asia, while Canadians would play a vital and often costly part in later European campaigns. More immediately, these nations kept Britain supplied with the resources it needed to fight on.

Within Europe, resistance networks were emerging to fight the Nazis. British covert operatives were smuggled onto the continent to provide them with arms and organizational help, but their acts of resistance, which included intelligence gathering, sabotage, and the assassination of Nazi officials, were carried out by local partisans risking death at the hands of a murderous regime.

From December 1940, America also began to play a more important part in the war. In a radio address to the nation, President Franklin D. Roosevelt set out his intention for America to become the "arsenal of democracy," providing the Allies in Europe with the military equipment they needed to fight against Germany and Italy. Roosevelt had to walk a delicate line. While he favored intervention in the war, many Americans preferred to maintain a policy of neutrality. The policy of arming free Europe, and to a lesser extent China, was a way of holding back imperial powers without committing America to a war it was not yet willing to fight.

One result of Roosevelt's decision was a rise in the importance of the Atlantic convoys. These merchant fleets, protected by military ships, were a vital lifeline for the British. They brought in not only war material manufactured in the United States but also a large part of the raw materials Britain needed to feed and arm itself. In

1941 alone, Britain imported 6.4 million metric tons of iron, steel, and iron ore, 13.1 million tons of oil, and 5.4 million tons of wheat. All of this despite the German submarines prowling the seas.

The successes of the Atlantic convoys, like so many other British successes in the war, were built in part upon ever-evolving intelligence work. Techniques in cryptography, aerial reconnaissance, human intelligence gathering, and analysis of the results took huge leaps forward. The cracking of the Enigma code, though important, was only one part in this great machine. Entire teams were dedicated to identifying and tracking German submarines. German advances in rocketry were followed. With the help of resistance operatives in Norway, the feared German battleship *Bismarck* was run to ground and sunk. Every single German spy in Britain was either imprisoned or turned into a double agent in the opening months of the war.

Meanwhile, Hitler was making plans to invade Britain. Operation Sealion would involve 43 German divisions crossing the Channel, surrounding London, and forcing the surrender of the British government.

This was no idle whim. Tanks were waterproofed and fitted with snorkels ready for amphibious landings. Artillery batteries were lined up along the French coast ready to bombard Britain. Ships and men were assembled.

As these preparations were underway, it became increasingly clear that Germany would need aerial superiority if it was to successfully cross the Channel. The German navy couldn't even clear mines without coming under attack from the Royal Air Force (RAF). Given the number of transport ships available, the Germans would have to cross in more than one wave, increasing their exposure to the RAF during that crossing.

So the Luftwaffe set out to gain control of the skies above Britain. Starting on August 8, 1940, hundreds of aircraft were launched every day to bomb British radar stations and airfields.

Around 1,300 German bombers and dive bombers were deployed in the Battle of Britain, along with 1,200 fighters to protect them. The RAF had around 600 fighters capable of front-line duty, most of them Hurricanes and Spitfires. Though most RAF pilots were British, some came from occupied countries. Four whole squadrons were manned by Poles and one by Czechs.

The Germans were confident, thanks to their superior numbers. But technologically, the Allies were at an advantage. At this stage in the war, their planes were generally better than those of the Germans, which included the Messerschmitt Bf 110 "destroyer," known by many as "Goering's folly" for its flawed design. The British also had a complete radar network covering their southern and eastern coastline, the most advanced radar network in the world. This let them see the Germans coming, get planes into the air to face them, and then direct those planes onto their targets.

For the first few months, the Germans focused on military installations. They attacked airbases, then ports and airfields, then radar stations, looking for the best way to cripple the RAF. Allied pilots were exhausted from constant combat, the RAF fighting on the edge of collapse.

All of this changed in August. On the 24th, a German plane accidentally dropped its bombs on civilian buildings in London. Prime Minister Winston Churchill ordered a retaliatory strike, and the next night British bombers hit Berlin. Hitler, who had promised his people that this would not happen, was furious. He shifted the Luftwaffe's focus off military targets and onto cities. Their aim was now to smash British industry and shred the enemy's morale through terror bombing.

Hundreds of tons of bombs fell nightly on London and other cities. The carnage was terrible, but it gave the RAF the rest they needed as attacks on their bases stopped. In mid-September, the balance of the fighting shifted. Now the Allies were destroying enemy planes faster than the Germans could make them. It became clear that the Germans were not going to win.

The bombing continued, but the risk of invasion looked vanishingly small.

While the air war hung in the balance, Operation Sealion was repeatedly postponed. Worsening weather made a cross-Channel invasion impossible until the spring. By the time better weather came around, Hitler had fixed his eyes on a new target.

Britain had survived its darkest hour.

Chapter 4 – Barbarossa Unleashed

In the years following the First World War, Germany and the USSR had had relatively cordial relations. The Soviets, alongside the Swedes, had helped the Germans to rebuild their military strength, in contravention of the terms of the Treaty of Versailles. German forces had even taken part in training operations in Russia, during which some of the lessons that led to Blitzkrieg were learned. In 1939, the Molotov-Ribbentrop Pact saw these two powerful nations agree to divide eastern Europe into separate spheres of influence and to maintain a state of non-aggression.

None of this meant anything to Hitler, despite his part in forging the pact. Communism was one of the hate figures upon which he had fixed, a bogey man that he considered a threat to the human spirit and to the new order he was building. He wanted to conquer the USSR to provide Germans with more living space, to further his agenda of wiping out Communists and Jews, and to increase Germany's strategic power through the land and raw resources this conquest would provide.

In December 1940, he signed a directive setting out his intention to "crush Soviet Russia in one rapid campaign."

He believed that, just like in Poland and France, German forces could overwhelm the enemy, conquering the USSR in three months through a blitzkrieg strike. The plan was titled Operation Barbarossa.

British and American intelligence learned in advance about Hitler's plan. In hopes of goading the Soviet leader, Josef Stalin, into acting against Hitler, they told him what they knew. But Stalin believed that Hitler would stand by the Molotov-Ribbentrop Pact. After all, the USSR was a great power and Germany already faced enemies to the west.

Over three million German soldiers, divided into 152 divisions, were mustered ready for the operation. Once again, the spearhead of the attack would be motorized forces, in the form of 17 panzer and 13 motorized infantry divisions. Nearly 2,000 Luftwaffe planes would support the advance.

Germany also brought in allies.

In 1940, following the partition of Poland, the USSR had occupied parts of Romania. Romania responded by allying itself with Germany and Italy. The Romanians sent 14 divisions to join Barbarossa, wanting an opportunity to take back their lost land.

The Finns were in a similar position, having lost territory to the Soviets during the Winter War. They supplied 17 divisions.

At 0530 on June 22, 1941, the German ambassador in Moscow delivered a declaration of war, claiming that the Soviets had violated the terms of the non-aggression pact.

Axis troops started advancing across a 1,900-mile long border that ran from the Black Sea to the Baltic.

In the early weeks of the operation, the Germans had the advantage. The Soviets had 150 divisions on the frontier and more coming to their aid, making them nearly a match in numbers. But the Germans were better trained and equipped. They had experience from fighting in Poland, Norway, Belgium, and France. While the Russians had more tanks and planes, the German ones were better. And while the Soviets had some capable commanders, they had also lost many to Stalin's purges, leaving the Germans at an advantage in experienced and skilled leadership.

Though only 20% of their troops were equipped for the lightning advance of Blitzkrieg, the Germans made swift advances. By the end of July, they swallowed up a stretch of the USSR twice as large as France. They surrounded entire Soviet armies and forced them to give up, including 600,000 soldiers at Minsk and Smolensk and another 665,000 at Kiev. They arrived in time to take in most of Ukraine's summer harvest, providing the Germans with food and just as critically taking it away from the Soviets. This happened despite Stalin's orders that, as when Napoleon had invaded 120 years before, the Russians should scorch the earth as they withdrew, depriving the invaders of supplies.

Food wasn't the only thing that the Germans were harvesting. The SS, the Nazi party's ideologically driven stormtroopers, made up a significant part of the advancing armies. Hitler had planned the campaign with their activities in mind. They immediately began murdering people the Nazis had singled out as inferior or objectionable: commissars, responsible for spreading and upholding communist ideology; Slavs, the majority population of parts of the USSR, who the Nazis considered degenerate; Jews, the most prominent scapegoats of Hitler's regime. At Baby Yar, 100,000 Ukrainian Jews were marched into a ravine north of the city and killed.

The brutality of the German occupation wasted one of the advantages they went in with—resentment at the Soviet regime. In the Baltic states, parts of Belorussia and areas of the Ukraine, they were initially welcomed as an alternative to Russian occupation or communist dictatorship. It is a cruel irony that the Jews of Kiev at first welcomed the Germans, who had treated them well during the First World War. But the murderous agenda of the Nazi party ensured that the new arrivals were soon seen as just more cruel invaders.

Based on the first few weeks, the Nazi commanders considered the invasion a huge success. They were driving the Soviets before them and wiping their opponents off the map. But bit by bit, the German advance slowed down. Two hundred more divisions of Soviet troops arrived, allowing Stalin to counter German training and technology with weight of numbers. Hitler's personal interventions led to some indecisive action on the part of the Germans, as the Führer switched between plans. A delay outside Leningrad allowed the Soviets to dig in there, beginning a siege that would last until 1944 and kill over 800,000 civilians. On the approach to Leningrad, the Finns halted their part of the war. They had retaken their lost territory and didn't want to invite future Soviet aggression by invading part of the USSR.

The power of Russian industry came into play. By the fall of Vyazma and Bryansk in October, they had only 824 tanks left on the front and no air support. But they had the capacity to rebuild. Stalin had built up an armaments industry based on quantity and uniformity, as opposed to the quality and variety that the Germans prized. This industrial machine could churn out massive numbers of tanks, planes, and supporting vehicles based on tractor designs. The USSR's population of farmers, who had been driving those same tractors for years, provided a ready pool of vehicle operatives, while millions of ordinary peasants were conscripted into an army of staggering scale.

To focus on quantity isn't to say that the Soviet equipment was necessarily bad. The T-34 tank, which the Germans faced in growing numbers, was perhaps the best tank of the war. It forced the Germans to develop new vehicles of their own. And the Russians kept churning them out. To keep production going, Stalin moved entire factories east, away from the German threat.

America and Britain played their part by providing materials for Russia's war effort. The British were eager to see the Axis occupied on another front, while the Americans saw this as an extension of the arsenal of democracy.

Then came the same force that had saved Russia from Napoleon in 1812—the winter. It was the coldest Russian winter for 140 years. Tanks became immobile as the oil froze in their engines. Artillery shells were stuck together as the grease they were packed in froze. Trenches could not be dug because of frozen ground. Frostbite hit the

German soldiers, whose uniforms were not warm enough for such terrible conditions.

As the latest advance on Moscow ground to a halt, the German army faced its opponents across a land of ice and snow.

Chapter 5 – Early Operations in Africa and the Mediterranean

Like Hitler, Mussolini had eyes on an eastern prize. While the Führer prepared for his war against the Soviet behemoth, his Italian ally was launching an offensive against a more vulnerable target in the form of Greece. This, together with Italian operations in North Africa, opened up the Mediterranean as a major theatre of war.

Italy's Mediterranean operations began while the Battle of France was still ongoing. In June 1940, they began a siege of the island of Malta, a relatively small target but one that was strategically important because of its position on supply routes through the Mediterranean. British and Commonwealth forces there held out against aerial bombing and naval blockades for the next two years.

After conquering British Somaliland in August, the Italians then began invasions of British-held Egypt in September and of Greece in October.

The Italians invaded Greece through Albania, which they had occupied just before the outbreak of the war. It was a campaign which was meant to prove that they were just as powerful as their German allies.

It ended up having the exact opposite effect. Seven Italian divisions were held up by a small force of Greeks, who drove them back out of the country and then went on the offensive. By the middle of December 1940, the Italians had lost a third of Albania. Meanwhile, the British and their Commonwealth allies offered the Greeks support, sending troops in to defend the country. This alarmed the Germans, as it put the Allies close to the Romanian oil fields, whose resources the German war machine desperately needed.

In North Africa, the Italians had colonial territory in Libya. To the east was Egypt, protected by British and Commonwealth troops, who were there to support the Egyptians and defend the Suez Canal, a vital transport route connecting the Mediterranean to the Indian Ocean. In mid-September 1940, the Italians crossed the border and advanced 50 miles into Egypt, occupying British bases.

The British and Indians countered in early December. Operation Compass, a five-day raid, drove the Italians out of Egypt. With Australian reinforcements, the British and Indians went on the attack, making decisive advances into Libya. They took the port of Tobruk, drove their opponents back 500 miles, and took 130,000 prisoners before the Italian 10th Army surrendered on February 7.

Meanwhile, the British Royal Navy had attacked the Italian fleet in harbor at Taranto. The Italians lost half their capital ships to a raid by torpedo bombers, severely hindering their ability to fight at sea.

By early 1941, things were looking bad for the Italians. They had been defeated and embarrassed on nearly every front. Hitler, fearful for the consequences if this continued, decided to step in. It was a move that would avert military disaster but do little to restore lost Italian dignity.

That spring, the German Afrika Corps arrived in Libya. It was led by General Rommel, one of the men who had led the German panzer divisions to such success in France. Rommel went on the offensive in March, driving the Allies back as far as the Egyptian border. They held on in Tobruk, which fell under siege by Axis forces for months. For the rest of the year, the war went back and forth, both sides experiencing a mixture of successes and defeats. The Allies were eventually able to relieve Tobruk and claim some victories, but Rommel had proven himself a challenging foe.

In March 1941, Bulgaria and Yugoslavia made alliances with the Axis powers. The Yugoslavian government was almost immediately overthrown by a British-backed coup. And so, in April, the Germans used their access to the region through Bulgaria to launch invasions of both Greece and Yugoslavia. Germany's fast-moving and powerful way of making war once again triumphed and both nations were conquered within a month.

British and Commonwealth forces retreated to the Greek island of Crete, allowing them to keep a foothold in the Balkans. But this didn't last. On May 20, the Germans launched the invasion of Crete, one of the most spectacular airborne operations in history. Paratroopers and glider-borne infantry swept across the island, overwhelming local partisans and Commonwealth forces. Despite some hard fighting, in which the soldiers of New Zealand played a prominent part, the Allies were forced to evacuate by the beginning of June.

For the major powers, the Balkans became a backwater of the war. But Yugoslavia remained a thorn in the German side throughout, as hard-fighting partisan forces launched persistent guerilla operations from hidden bases in the hills.

Further east, challenges in the Middle East threatened the British eastern flank in Egypt. Syria and Lebanon were controlled by Vichy French forces. In April 1941, a coup put a pro-Axis government in charge of Iraq.

The British and Commonwealth troops responded with a swift campaign to regain control of Iraq, where they had military bases before the war. Having installed a puppet government favorable to them, they moved on to invade the Vichy-held territories and so shore up their position in North Africa. This time they were assisted by Free French forces. The Vichy troops put up strong resistance, but the whole campaign was still over in less than a month, ending in victory for the Allies.

In Africa, the strategies of both sides were dictated in large part by supply lines. It was hard to support extended lines across the desert and so the British withdrew a little in January 1942.

Rommel responded by going on the offensive. In a series of attacks, he pushed the Allied forces back. In June, he beat them at the Battle of Gazala. Tobruk was surrounded and surrendered to Axis forces in June, as the Allies could no longer supply the port for an extended siege.

In July, the Allies drove off a series of German attacks in the First Battle of El Alamein, halting Rommel's advance. He attacked again at the end of August, but was defeated by the British under their new commander, General Bernard Montgomery, at the Battle of Alam el Halfa. This had been Rommel's last chance to overrun Egypt before more troops arrived to bolster the Allies. From now on, the tide of war would turn against him.

Montgomery's presence also played a part in turning the tide of war. In October, he led the British and Commonwealth troops in a fresh offensive, defeating Rommel at the Second Battle of El Alamein.

Rommel began a steady retreat east. This was done despite orders from Hitler, who commanded him to hold his ground. This became a recurring theme as the war turned against Germany. Hitler would order his commanders to fight on no matter what, not surrendering territory to the enemy. They, realizing the need for tactical retreats, would face the choice between challenging their leader, disobeying him, or carrying out orders they knew to be futile.

Rommel pulled back east while Montgomery steadily advanced. The German commander sometimes sacrificed his infantry to preserve his more valuable armored forces. By the end of 1942, they were halfway across Libya and heading for Tunisia, another Axis-controlled territory. But by then the whole shape of the war had changed.

The Americans were coming.

Chapter 6 – A Day Which Will Live in Infamy

While war raged in Europe and North Africa, Japanese actions in East Asia were setting in motion the events that would turn this into a global war.

In September 1940, Japan signed a treaty with Germany and Italy, bringing it into the alliance known as the Axis. Though Japan was not committed to fighting at their side, it was showing where its allegiances lay.

Meanwhile, the war in China raged on. The American government provided support to Chiang Kai-Shek and the nationalist forces resisting the Japanese invasion, as well as imposing sanctions on Japan. American troops might not be there on the ground, but it was another intervention by Western powers against a nation that already resented their presence.

Hitler's successes in Europe forced the Japanese government's hand. They wanted to take control of the European colonies in Asia. If they waited too long and the Germans seized control of Europe, Hitler's government would then lay claim to the colonies of the nations they had conquered. Japan needed to deal with China and grab those colonies before it was too late.

In November 1941, the Japanese sent the US an ultimatum, demanding that it lift its embargo, stop supporting the Chinese, and start selling the Japanese the oil they needed to power their war machine. The Americans were just as cornered diplomatically as the Japanese. If they gave in then Britain would lose the raw resources of its empire, the Axis would dominate in Europe, and the USA would be faced on all sides by hostile powers. So America refused to accede to the demands.

On December 7, 1941, Japan launched a surprise attack on the American naval base at Pearl Harbor in the Hawaiian Islands. It was primarily an air attack, using bombers launched from Japanese aircraft carriers, though submarines were also involved.

Devastating as the attack was, it did not achieve its goal. The American aircraft carriers were not in port and so these vital resources were not hit by the attack.

This was not the only attack launched by the Japanese that day. They also invaded Hong Kong, Guam, Wake Island, Midway, and the Philippines, where a large American force fought a fighting retreat before being cut off and forced to surrender. The Japanese were making a huge grab for power.

Though negotiations had been increasingly tense over the previous month, the Americans considered the Pearl Harbor attack to be a great break from diplomatic protocol, as it was not preceded by a declaration of war. President Roosevelt labeled December 7 as "a day which will live in infamy." The American public was outraged. The following day, the government declared war against Japan, with only a single congressman voting against the declaration. Isolationism, so long the bedrock of American foreign policy, had been decisively smashed.

Britain joined the Americans in declaring war on Japan. British territory was being invaded and Britain and the Commonwealth had the resources to play a meaningful part in the war, despite commitments in Europe and Africa.

Over the following days, Japan continued to occupy small territories around its sphere of influence. On December 10, Japanese forces sank the HMS *Prince of Wales* and the HMS *Repulse*, the two most powerful British warships in the region. The Japanese were riding high on a wave of success.

The relationship between Germany and Japan was not a close one. When the Germans declared war on the USSR, Japan declined to join them. Though Japan and the Soviets were rivals who had fought in the past, the Japanese were happy to see their opponents distracted and saw no need to join in. But on December 11, Hitler came out in support of Japan by declaring war on the US. It was a move that ensured that America would commit to the war in Europe, not just Asia. America responded by declaring war on Germany and Italy.

The diplomatic fallout from Pearl Harbor turned separate conflicts in Europe and Asia into a single war that circled the globe.

America quickly began gearing up for war. Young men rushed to join the armed forces. Boatloads of freshly recruited marines began journeys across the Pacific, the ships taking winding routes to avoid Japanese submarines. Both sides knew that aircraft carriers would be critical to the conflict and so many naval pilots also had to be recruited. The military industry expanded to produce vast quantities of munitions, weapons, vehicles, and other supplies.

One of Japan's most important objectives was to take Australia. As part of the Commonwealth, the Australians were a major source of troops for the British. They were also friendly trading partners with America. Australia would provide a southern anchor to island territories scattered across the western Pacific.

The Japanese worked their way south toward Australia, swallowing territory as they went. The East Indies, Guam, and Wake Island all became part of their empire. Soon, they would have the bases they needed to cut off supply lines between Australia and the USA.

The first major battle between Japanese and Allied forces took place in May 1942. An American fleet, with some Australian support, took on the Japanese in a battle of great historical significance. For the first time ever, two fleets fought without their ships even seeing each other. The engagement was decided entirely by air power, as planes from aircraft carriers attacked the opposing fleets.

The Battle of the Coral Sea was not a decisive encounter. The Japanese did more damage than the Allies but suffered losses that would hamper them in the next fleet battle. Strategically, it was the first time that a Japanese advance had been halted. In that sense, it was an important symbolic moment.

The more militarily decisive moment came a month later. A Japanese fleet was heading toward Midway Island, which was defended by American aircraft and ground forces. If the Japanese took Midway, they could use it as a base from which to launch attacks on Pearl Harbor, threatening America's ability to act in the western Pacific.

As the Japanese approached Midway, they were attacked by planes from the island and from an American fleet coming up behind them. Though the Japanese pilots in their Zero fighters performed well, it was not enough to win. They lost four aircraft carriers, which the Japanese could ill afford to replace, while the Americans, who were already working on more ships, lost only one carrier. The invasion force was turned back and the Americans gained a decisive advantage at sea. The tide of war was about to turn.

While this was going on, another front opened up that would see Japanese ground forces in constant conflict with the Allies for the rest of the war. In December 1941, the Japanese and their Thai allies invaded Burma, a part of the British Empire. There, they drove back British forces, including those from imperial India, and Chinese troops. They were initially very successful, occupying most of Burma. But it was a success that would stall, creating a fighting front that would last for the rest of the war.

Chapter 7 – Germany's Eastern Offensives

In Europe, most fighting was still taking place on the Eastern front, where German military faced the massive industrial and human resources of the Soviet Union.

One of the greatest mistakes Hitler made was underestimating how much material, both human and industrial, Stalin could bring to the war. Without even the distraction of war with Japan, he could draw in the military resources of the eastern provinces of the USSR. Even as fresh materials were being made and new soldiers recruited, existing troops were flowing west ready to face the invaders.

The first serious Soviet counter-offensive took place in the winter of 1941-2. The Germans had been held up outside Moscow. Now was the time to drive them back and remove the threat to the Soviet capital.

The offensive began on December 5. The Soviets had only a slight edge over the Germans in numbers, but by careful deployment they were able to outnumber them two to one at significant points along the front.

The offensive progressed slowly at first but built up some momentum. Solnechnogorsk and Klin were recaptured. The Germans were forced into a retreat.

German commanders wanted to make tactical withdrawals to save their forces, but Hitler would not let them. Arguments behind the scenes saw upheaval in the senior ranks of the army and men disobeying orders. After much disruption, limited withdrawals were finally allowed.

The Soviets tried several times to surround and destroy parts of the invading force. The German Third Panzer Army and then the Second Panzer Army both escaped such traps. XXXIX Corps was surrounded and destroyed while buying time for others to retreat.

With freezing weather interfering with German planes, the Soviets matched their opponents in the skies for the first time. But the Luftwaffe still helped to keep the German army alive, providing air cover as troops pulled back.

After a month of progress, the Soviet offensive ran out of steam. The battle lines settled down. Soviet troops had driven the Germans back for the first time. Moscow looked far safer than it had a month before.

The Soviets launched another counter-attack in the spring. This time, it ended in disaster. Two Siberian divisions were encircled by the Germans outside Leningrad. A tank force punched through the Romanian Sixth Army, only to be surrounded by the Germans. Six hundred tanks and a quarter of a million men fell into Axis hands.

As the weather improved, the Germans prepared to launch a fresh offensive. Called Case Blue, this time their plan was focused not on the Soviet heartland but on the Baku oil fields in the south. This would provide the Germans with vital supplies of fuel, depriving the Soviets of the same resources. It would also threaten British India.

Case Blue was a two-pronged offensive. Army Group A advanced across the Caucasus Mountains and into the oil fields. To their north, Army Group B protected their flank through an advance toward the city of Stalingrad.

The offensive began in late June. Army Group A made slow progress toward its goal. Many of the troops being used were not suited to mountain warfare. The further they progressed, the more problems arose with getting supplies to them, due to the logistical challenges of long supply lines in difficult terrain. Progress toward the oil fields ground to a halt.

When it became clear that the Germans were not going to take the oil fields for themselves, Hitler decided on another option. If they couldn't have the oil then they could at least stop the Soviets from using it. The Luftwaffe began a bombing campaign aimed at destroying the oil infrastructure. But again, the Germans fell short of their goals. They could only reach some of the refineries by direct routes, meaning that the Soviets could tell where the bombers would be coming. As more Soviet planes reached the region and the Germans had to draw some of theirs off to fight elsewhere, it became clear that the oil fields were not going to be taken out. The Germans had hampered the Soviets' ability to fuel themselves but not struck the decisive blow they had hoped for.

Army Group B began its main advance in late July, heading toward the River Don. In most places, they were able to push the Soviets back across the river, but some bridgeheads remained, threatening the Axis forces.

On August 23, the Germans crossed the Don, establishing their own bridgehead on the far side. On the same day, German forces reached the outskirts of Stalingrad, beginning one of the most bitterly fought battles of the war. After the Soviet 62nd Army was almost encircled by German forces, the Soviets retreated elsewhere on the front. Stalingrad become the focal point of the whole offensive.

The Battle of Stalingrad was one of the bloodiest in the history of war. Nearly two million people were killed, wounded, or captured in the fighting. It was the ruin of German ambitions in Russia.

For the first three months, Axis forces were on the offensive. While other Axis troops, including Romanians and Hungarians, guarded their flanks, the Germans launched a devastating assault on the city. Artillery and bombers pounded away while troops advanced through the ruined streets.

Here, the Germans could not use the fast-flowing blitzkrieg tactics that had stood them in good stead elsewhere. They became bogged down in street fighting, to which the Soviets swiftly adjusted. Though Axis forces continued to make progress for three months, capturing most of the city west of the Volga, it cost them dearly. Russian soldiers held out in isolated pockets long after the Germans had passed by, meaning that nowhere was secure. Nowhere felt safe.

One German veteran said that "The streets are no longer measured in meters, but in corpses."

On November 19, the Soviets launched a counter-attack. Rather than face the Germans in the city head on, they attacked to the north and south. They punched through the weaker Axis forces holding the flanks and surrounded the German army.

The roles had been reversed and now the Germans were the ones under siege. As a Soviet offensive drove Axis forces back elsewhere and those at Stalingrad tightened their grip, the German Sixth Army became increasingly isolated and short of supplies. As was his way, Hitler would not allow them to surrender despite the desperate circumstances. They had no hope of winning. At last, on February 2, 1943, the last German forces in Stalingrad were defeated. The mighty Sixth Army had been lost, along with all its veteran troops.

Soviet confidence received a massive boost, while German morale plummeted. As the Germans and their allies were pushed back, the Kursk Salient developed—a bulge in the lines near Kursk, in which Soviet troops had pushed back the Germans. The Germans responded by developing their last great offensive on the Eastern Front—Operation Citadel.

The fundamental point of Citadel was simple. Axis forces would advance from north and south into the neck of the Kursk Salient, joining up to cut off the Soviet troops there. It would allow them to destroy a significant part of the Soviet armed forces and retake the offensive.

But the Soviets had also been making plans, preparing counter-offensives for just such an occasion. Warned about the German plans by British intelligence, they prepared a defense in depth for the salient.

In July 1943, the Germans launched their operation, triggering a fresh period of intense fighting. The war in the Mediterranean meant that they did not have all the resources the commanders hoped for, but they still thought that there was a chance for victory.

The Battle of Kursk is best remembered for large tank clashes, including the Battle of Prokhorovka, one of the largest tank battles in history. Up and down the lines, the Soviets held up the German attacks, robbing them of the decisive victory that they needed. After a week and a half, the German offensive ended, to be replaced by Soviet offensives. It became clear that the Germans would not achieve what Hitler wanted and Citadel was called off. It was a victory for the Soviets.

Stalingrad was the turning point on the Eastern Front, but Kursk ended German hopes for another reversal. The invasion begun with Operation Barbarossa had turned into a grinding mess which was eating up German resources in a series of failed offensives. Things were about to get even worse for Hitler's armies, as the Russians gained the initiative and went on the attack.

Chapter 8 – Guadalcanal and the War in Asia

The Germans weren't the only Axis power losing the initiative in the war. In the Pacific, the tide of Japanese expansion was about to be halted and then reversed as the Allies went on the offensive.

The Allied offensive began on New Guinea, a large island territory to the north of Australia. It had several advantages as a starting point. It would be easy to support troops there, thanks to the proximity of the Allied fleets. It would also be easy to move in supplies, given how close it was to the Australian mainland. And the Japanese had already been halted there.

The Japanese had originally landed in New Guinea on the north side of the island. A guerilla campaign had contained them there in the area around Salamaua. An invasion force had been prepared to land at Port Moresby, on the south side of the island, giving the Japanese overall control. But this fleet was halted by the lack of a clear Japanese victory in the Battle of the Coral Sea. Meanwhile, Australian troops, supported by a smaller force of Americans, were assembling on the south side of the island.

July and August 1942 saw clashes between the Allies and newly arrived Japanese troops. Australian forces conducted a fighting retreat, during which they gained valuable experience of jungle fighting. Extended supply lines and Allied air attacks hampered the Japanese advance. Finally, in late September, the Allies began their own offensive.

Over the next year, they launched a series of successful attacks against the Japanese. Time and again, the Allies inflicted far heavier casualties than they received. Through a combination of cross-country marches and amphibious landings, they repeatedly isolated Japanese troops, forcing them to retreat or hold out in tiny enclaves. As the Japanese lost their supply lines and troops sent to reinforce them were lost at sea, their situation became increasingly desperate.

But while the Japanese never regained the initiative, they never gave up; 13,500 Japanese soldiers held on in New Guinea until they surrendered at the end of the war.

Meanwhile, the Americans began their main campaign with the battle that made the name of the US Marine Corps.

Guadalcanal was a British possession in the Solomon Islands. In July 1942, Japanese troops landed there and began building an airstrip. To prevent the Japanese gaining a base for air power in the region, the Americans hastily threw together an invasion force of Marines.

They landed on August 7 and took the airfield the next day, giving them a base of operations. The Japanese had withdrawn into the jungle rather than face the full weight of the invasion force. The Marines hurriedly finished work on the airfield so that their own planes could land.

Control of the seas around Guadalcanal was vital. The Japanese at first had the naval advantage, letting them bombard the American ground troops using planes and naval guns. For three months, the Americans and Australians could not risk sending in ships to support the Marines.

In November, the Allies finally got a naval victory, sinking two Japanese battleships. They took control of the waters around Guadalcanal, ensuring that they received the supplies they needed and that the Japanese were deprived of theirs.

On the island, the Marines had dug in around the airfield, from which an air group gave them the best support it could with limited resources. The Americans saw for the first time how the Japanese fought, including the unsettling banzai charges, hundreds of men racing fearlessly at the enemy gun lines. The fighting was often fierce, the Japanese launching desperate charges that ended in heavy casualties and sometimes brutal hand-to-hand combat, men killing each other up close.

One of the darkest elements of the fighting was the behavior of wounded Japanese soldiers. Rather than surrender to the Americans, they would often lie quietly until the victors came to check on them, then make suicidal attacks. As a result, American soldiers started shooting or stabbing corpses rather than risk them turning out to still be alive and ready to attack. The Japanese unwillingness to accept the dishonor of capture or defeat was changing their opponents as well as them.

The horrors of Guadalcanal weren't just about the fighting. Dysentery and malaria took their toll, as did shortages of supplies and sleep, night watches and shore bombardments robbing men of their rest.

But the same problems faced the Japanese, who were having no luck driving back the Americans. Their government finally grew weary of their losses. In February, they secretly withdrew their troops from the island, leaving it to the Americans.

While Guadalcanal was the most important and protracted fight the Americans were engaged in, it wasn't the only one. In February 1943, they landed on the Russell Islands. A campaign of air attacks in the Aleutians from August 1942 led to an invasion in May 1943, in which they seized control of the islands, putting them within bombing range of Japan. A series of operations in and around New Britain led to the isolation of the large Japanese force at Rabaul, letting the Allies bypass this army rather than having to take it on.

Meanwhile, the fight for Burma continued. The British, including imperial troops from India, tried to hold out against Japanese aggression and even go on the offensive. But they weren't prepared for much of what the Japanese threw at them, including offensives through supposedly impassable jungle that turned the Allied flank. Two small Allied offensives during the dry season proved ineffective and they were forced to withdraw toward the Indian border.

One of the problems the British faced was the state of India. This was their most solid base in the region and it was becoming increasingly unstable. Famine in Bengal added to already growing resentment of British rule. Troops had to be committed to keeping the peace, reducing the forces that could be sent into Burma.

In the jungles and steep hills of Burma, the British developed new ways of fighting. Much of this was based on the techniques of guerilla warfare, developed into a new military doctrine by innovators such as Orde Wingate. His Chindit irregulars used long marches and air drops to penetrate deep behind the Japanese lines, with the aim of disrupting their communications and supplies. They used the jungle to their advantage, trying to stay away from places where the Japanese could bring tanks and heavy artillery to bear. The practical effectiveness of the Chindits was limited, whether through faults in Wingate's thinking or due to the intervention of officers who disagreed with his approach. But their bold campaigns unsettled the Japanese and boosted the morale of Allied forces in the region.

The British also worked on recruiting local forces to resist the Japanese. Special operatives went behind the lines to recruit local tribes and former Burma Rifles, ready to rise up against the Japanese when the time came. As in Europe, the Allies kept their enemies stretched thin by supporting resistance to their rule.

Japanese rule in the Pacific was particularly harsh. Brutal punishment of dissidents and captured enemy combatants was common. Thousands of Allied servicemen died in terrible conditions in prison, as did Western civilians herded into camps in occupied territories. This was not the systematic extinction that would eventually be revealed in Europe, but an imperial regime willing to use cruel tactics to achieve its aims. No nation emerged from the war with clean hands, but the Japanese earned a particularly terrible reputation among their neighbors.

Chapter 9 – Operation Torch and the Taking of North Africa

Though Japanese aggression had drawn America into immediate fighting in the Pacific, this was not the strategic priority for any of the main players in the Allied camp. Europe was their priority, and the American government was keen to get involved. American planes and pilots went to join the British in their bombardment of German cities, attacks which struck the same terror into the Germans that they had inflicted upon London and the industrial cities of England. But what the Americans really wanted was to put boots on the ground.

The American government's preferred option was to launch an invasion of mainland Europe. Churchill convinced them that this should not be their starting point. First, they would defeat the Axis in north Africa and the Mediterranean. Then they could make a move on France.

Out of this strategic decision, Operation Torch was born. This was an Anglo-American operation, with the Americans providing the bulk of the forces while the British brought their experience and knowledge of the war in North Africa.

Operation Torch began on November 8, 1942. Over 100,000 personnel made three separate seaborne landings at different points along the coast of northwest Africa, all targeted territory held by the Vichy French. The furthest east would position the Allies to threaten the Germans in Tunisia.

The Torch landings were generally a success. The French response was mixed, some resisting while others gladly went over to the Allied side. Within days, the Allies had a solid foothold in Africa.

Having established themselves, the Allies began a campaign to conquer Tunisia. The ports of Tunis and Bizerte were particularly critical, as these were the main harbors remaining to the Axis forces. Rommel and the Afrika Corps were already retreating in the face of Montgomery's troops in the east. If they could be cut off the west and deprived of their escape route then it would be a huge victory for the Allies.

The advance wasn't an easy one. Supply lines had to be arranged across hundreds of miles of Algerian desert. The first attempt to take Tunisia, by the British First Army, was repulsed by a strong German force including air support from the Luftwaffe, who had bases close to the front line.

In December, a second attempt on Tunis also met with failure. American, British, and French forces struggled to work together in difficult and unfamiliar conditions. Air support for the Allies was not as good as for the Axis forces. The advance made it as far as Longstop Hill, a high point with good views of the ground toward Tunis, and the two sides fought for the hill for four days over Christmas.

But the attempt to reach Tunis failed. Then came rainy weather, turning the ground to mud, and further advances had to be postponed.

Tensions were high in the Allied armies as they sat out the winter of 1942-3. The British had more experience of war, not just from this one but from their long history as a colonial power. The Americans, on the other hand, were confident and outspoken, the representatives of a superpower on the rise. The British found the Americans boastful despite their inexperience. The Americans found the British cold and patronizing. There were bar fights between the soldiers and tense arguments among the high command.

In January 1943, Montgomery reached Tripoli. There he stopped to rest and repair before he continued his pursuit of Rommel.

Rommel took the opportunity to create a defensive position on the Mareth Line, where he believed that he could hold the British up with minimal resources. This would give him the freedom to attack the less experienced forces to the west.

On February 14, Rommel launched his attack against American forces at Sidi Bou Zid in the strategically important Faid Pass. He routed the Americans and then drove off their hastily assembled counter-attack.

From the Faid Pass, Rommel moved on to the Kasserine Pass. Here, he was held up by British forces, which fought a careful delaying action as they retreated from the German assault. Though Rommel won control of the pass, he had lost momentum, left his flank exposed, and over-extended his supply lines. The advance could not be maintained.

Instead, Rommel turned east, attacking Montgomery at Medenine. The British commander was used to his opponent's tactics and prepared a good defensive position, with British and New Zealand troops firing on the flank of Rommel's force as it advanced. The Germans were soundly defeated. Rommel was summoned home by Hitler, leaving the African troops in the hands of the more cautious Von Arnim.

Meanwhile, American morale declined. They had not yet had a significant victory and British successes were only making their allies more arrogant. Something had to change.

The first thing to go was one of the American commanders, General Fredendall, an indecisive leader whose hostility to the British had contributed to tensions among the commanders. He was replaced by General George Patton, one of the most colorful, bold, and abrasive characters of the war. Patton's new deputy was Omar Bradley, who in a quieter way would also prove to be one of America's best commanders.

While the Germans retreated west, British officers set up training programs to better prepare American troops. It wasn't a popular move, given that it played into the image of British superiority, but it helped to toughen the men up for the coming fight.

Shortly after taking command of his part of the frontline forces, Patton launched an attack that took the airfield at Gafsa. When Von Arnim launched a counter-attack,

Patton's troops again defeated the Germans at the Battle of El Guettar. It wasn't a massive engagement, but it was a symbolically important one. It proved to the British that the Americans could hold their own.

Montgomery went back on the offensive in March, launching an attack on the Mareth Line. A direct assault by the British was driven off after 24 hours of heavy fighting. But the New Zealand Corps, with support from the air and from other British troops, made a flanking maneuver that broke through the enemy lines. The Axis forces retreated ten miles then made another stand, inflicting heavy casualties on the British. At last the Germans retreated again, until they were only 50 miles from the port of Tunis.

With an eye to what would follow after Africa, the Allies tried to cut off the retreat of the Axis forces. This led to failure at Fondouk Pass for an American force under General Ryder. The result was yet more arguing among the Allies, as Patton blamed the British air support and the British air commander blamed the quality of the American troops. General Eisenhower, the American officer in overall command of the Allied forces, ended up ordering an apology out of the outraged British commander.

Divisions continued as General Alexander drew up the plan for the final campaign. It gave the lead to the British, with the Americans taking only a minor role. Under pressure from politicians back home and commanders in the field, Eisenhower persuaded Alexander to change his plan. The Americans would take Bizerte.

The attack on Bizerte provided redemption for Ryder, the embarrassed commander from Fondouk Pass. Following five days of fighting, his infantry and armor launched a combined assault that took control of the critical Hill 609. They then fought off a series of counter-attacks.

American forces also broke through the defenses of Bizerte, cutting off any Axis escape.

When Hitler refused to send more supplies, Von Arnim found himself in an impossible position. He surrendered on May 12, along with 150,000 troops.

The Allies now controlled North Africa, and with it the southern Mediterranean. Though tensions remained between the different nations, the Americans had gained vital experience and prestige. The time was fast approaching for them to do what they had wanted from the start.

The Western Allies were about to invade Europe.

Chapter 10 – The Tide Turns in Eastern Europe

On the Eastern Front, the balance of the war had shifted decisively in favor of the Soviets. Germany's best hope had always lain in a decisive strike that would cripple the USSR. In Poland and France, this had been achieved in a matter of weeks. In North Africa, the greatest successes had come not from a slow grind but from swift actions that caught the Allies off guard. But in the USSR, that swift strike had not brought the results the Germans needed. Instead of knocking out the Soviet military machine and taking key cities, the Germans had become bogged down in fighting that had now lasted over two years.

In a war of attrition, the Soviets had the edge thanks to their large population and high-volume approach to armaments production. The Germans could counter the T-34 tank with their own Tigers and Panthers, but they couldn't make as much materiel as the Soviets. Weight of numbers and Soviet tenacity had thwarted German ambitions.

In the summer of 1943, the Soviets began a counter-offensive on multiple fronts. This began with an advance on the Orel salient, where German forces had been holding out since their failure to reach Moscow during Operation Barbarossa. Further south, the Soviets broke through positions around Belgorod and advanced on Kharkov. A war of movement saw the Soviets get around the Germans' flank, forcing them to pull back. By the end of August, both Orel and Kharkov had been retaken.

Hitler at last allowed his forces to pull back to the Dnieper river. Here, the Germans had planned to build a defensive line like the fortifications on their border with France. But these fortifications had not yet been built, and so the German forces found themselves trying to hold a position that had not been prepared.

The Soviets pressed relentlessly on. Though an attempt to get around the German lines with paratroopers failed, other forces got across the Dnieper and formed bridgeheads, forcing the Germans back. Hitler insisted that his generals cling to the Dnieper line.

A counterattack by German Panzer troops briefly held up the Soviets west of Kiev. But it wasn't enough to form a solid line. Panzer divisions were repeatedly surrounded by Soviet troops and had to make costly breakouts to avoid capture.

In the north, the Soviets made little effort to advance until January 1944. When it came, the shock of the Soviet attack sent the Germans reeling. They were driven back from Leningrad. Novgorod was retaken. The Soviets pushed toward the Baltic Sea, hoping to use it to threaten Germany's eastern territories. Soon, they were at the border of Estonia, where some locals joined up to fight for the Germans rather than suffer a second Soviet occupation.

By now, Stalin was working in cooperation with the Western Allies. Together, they decided on a massive Russian offensive in Belarus, to coincide with the Anglo-American invasion of Western Europe.

By the time the attack was launched on June 22, 1944, German troops had already been stripped from the east to man the new Western front. Massive Soviet forces faced weakened German lines and their superiority in numbers quickly brought victory. Within a month, they had reached the Polish border. By the end of August, the Germans had lost 400,000 dead, wounded, or missing, while the Russians had lost less than half that number.

In July, another offensive was launched in the south. Western Ukraine was retaken. From there, Soviet forces pressed on into Romania. A coup there replaced the Axis-oriented government, leading to peace between Russia and Romania in September.

Meanwhile, a fresh offensive was launched against Finland. Just like in the Winter War, the Soviets found the Finns tougher opponents than they had anticipated. Though they quickly broke through the first two lines of Finnish defenses, the Finns retreated, regrouped, and held them at a third line.

Though the Finns were holding off the Soviets for now, they knew that it could not last. In September, the Finns made peace with the Russians, agreeing to an armistice that included punitive payments to the victors. As part of the agreement, German troops had to be hastily evacuated from Finland, harassed by their former allies along the way.

This deprived the Germans of important mineral resources that had been coming out of Finland.

As the Soviets approached Poland, local forces rose up against the Germans. The Polish Home Army, one of the largest and most organized resistance networks in Europe, launched Operation Tempest. This was a series of risings meant to coincide with the approach of Soviet troops, so that the Poles could join with them in defeating the Germans. The aim was both to drive out the Nazis and to establish an independent Polish government before the Soviets could take over.

Stalin, seeing the dual aims of Tempest, held his forces back. In the most infamous incident, a massive rising in Warsaw was put down by the Germans after Soviet troops failed to come to the aid of the Poles.

Similar events took place further south. The Slovak National Uprising, launched in August 1944, tried to overthrow the government collaborating with the Nazis in occupied Slovakia and to throw out the Germans. Though the insurgency was largely put down, it marked the beginning of a period of increased guerilla operations by the Slovaks, which continued until Allies forces reached their country in 1945.

In September 1944, the Soviets launched a series of operations along the northern stretch of the Eastern Front, known collectively as the Baltic Offensive. They drove back the German forces occupying Estonia and Lithuania. The remains of the German Army Group North were cut off from the rest of the German forces, contained in a shrinking pocket of territory on the Baltic coast. Hundreds of thousands of German soldiers and civilians were trapped, living in fear of how they would be treated when the Soviet army arrived.

There was good reason for many of them to fear. The Soviets were embittered not just by invasion and years of war but also by the murderous behavior of the German SS in occupied territories. The soldiers of the Red Army had seen how barbarously their people had been treated. The desire for revenge, stoked by Soviet propaganda, fueled hatred of the Germans.

In January 1945, the Soviets finally entered Warsaw. The city was in ruins, destroyed both by the war and by the Germans as an act of punishment for Polish resistance. Soviet forces were already pushing south from Poland into Slovakia. Now, as they headed east, they reached Germany itself.

Launched in January 1945, the Vistula-Oder offensive was a remarkable achievement. Outnumbering the Germans they faced by five or six to one, the Soviets punched their way east, sometimes advancing over twenty miles in a day. They took control of the remaining Baltic states and East Prussia. Along the way, they suffered 194,000 casualties. When the operation was called to a halt in February, they were on the River Oder, less than 50 miles from Berlin.

By early 1945, the German armed forces were in ruins across Eastern Europe. From his hidden command bunkers, Hitler sent out orders for the reorganization of armies, for counter-offensives, for defensive lines to be held. But Axis resources were stretched thin, as the Allies made advances on other fronts. Around the world, the war had shifted against Hitler and his allies.

Chapter 11 – Advancing on Japan

A critical change in the tide of war in the Pacific was also seen in 1943. In the early stages, the Japanese had steadily advanced down the long chain of islands separating the Pacific from the Indian Ocean. Now the flow was reversed. Having halted the Japanese at Guadalcanal, the Allies began driving them north.

One of the first offensive operations happened further out into the Pacific, in the Gilbert Islands. There, the American Admiral Nimitz launched a seaborne invasion in November 1943. Makin was easily captured but Tarawa proved more challenging. One thousand US Marines were killed and another 2,100 wounded taking a tiny cluster of islands from the Japanese. The losses shocked the American public, but in the long term the problems faced at Tarawa saved lives. They taught vital lessons about how to carry out an amphibious assault, lessons which would be applied in the invasion of Normandy the following summer.

Next to fall were the Marshall Islands. Here, the Japanese dug in in an attempt to tie up Allied troops and supply chains. Heavy bombardments by American ships softened up Japanese positions ready for the attacks, providing

Allied troops with easier landings when they arrived in January 1944. The Japanese base at Truk in the Carolines came under particularly heavy bombardment to keep it from supporting the Japanese elsewhere.

In June, the Allies began invading the Marianas. The invasion of Saipan set the tone for this fighting, as the Japanese dug in, using caves and bunkers to protect them from the American bombardment. Troops had to take them out one strongpoint at a time, an exhausting business that strained men's morale and cost heavy casualties. The same tactics would be repeated as the Japanese clung to their conquests all the way up the western Pacific. At every stage, the Allies became bogged down dealing with smaller and smaller pockets of resistance.

While the battle for Saipan was still raging, Admiral Jisaburo Ozawa tried to counter American advances. On June 19, he attacked the American 5th Fleet in the Battle of the Philippine Sea. Ozawa had nine aircraft carriers to the Americans' fifteen and was relying on support from land-based aircraft. But those planes had already been put out of action by Allied raids. The Americans destroyed the waves of Japanese planes sent against them. Their submarines and bombers destroyed many of the Japanese carriers. The Japanese withdrew with heavy losses.

In the skies, the Allies now dominated. They had a huge advantage in aircraft carriers. Their planes, though not always as agile as the Japanese fighters, were generally sturdier. With the fall of Saipan, they were able to establish an air base within bomber range of the Japanese mainland.

On November 12, 1944, a flight of 100 bombers set out on the first air raid against Tokyo since the symbolic Doolittle Raid of 1942. This time, the bombers meant business. Over the months that followed, bombs would devastate Japanese cities, bringing the sort of ruin previously seen in Europe.

The value of such bombing has been seriously questioned since the war. In Britain in particular, Bomber Command clung to the tactics of terror bombing, aiming to smash enemy industry and morale. This was done despite the evidence about its effectiveness, not because of it. But the ability of the Americans to strike at Japan certainly unsettled the government there. Following the fall of Saipan, the entire cabinet resigned. To many in government, defeat looked increasingly inevitable.

In July 1944, US Marines invaded the island of Guam, the first American territory seized by the Japanese in 1941. Despite fierce Japanese counter-attacks, they took the island through a month of hard fighting. Only ten miles long and thirty miles wide, Guam cost the Americans 1,440 men dead, 145 missing, and 5,648 wounded; 10,693 Japanese died. When the island fell, many of the rest fled into the jungle to fight on. One of them did not emerge until 1972.

Tinian, the last significant part of the Marianas, fell more easily. A surprise attack by US Marines from Saipan established a beachhead on the island. Within a week, they had taken out the entire Japanese garrison.

The desperate fighting of the Japanese unsettled the Americans. But the real cost of such tactics fell upon Japan. In the fighting for the Marianas, they lost almost ten times as many men dead or captured as their enemies were killed.

The next stop in the American advance was a symbolically important one—the Philippines. The Philippines had been held by American forces when the Japanese invaded in 1941. Thousands of American servicemen had been taken prisoner when the islands fell. General MacArthur, who had been in charge of defending the Philippines, was now in charge of American forces fighting in the Pacific and was determined to make good his promise to return to the islands.

The Americans began their invasion of the Philippines in October 1944, when troops landed on Leyte and nearby islands. The Japanese responded by launching a plan named Sho-Go or Operation Victory. This was the last great effort by the Japanese navy to keep the American threat away from their homeland and to protect the oil supplies that would keep the fleet in action. To do this, they sent naval forces toward Leyte in three separate groups, with the aim of hitting the Allied invasion force with heavy air attacks. But American and Australian fleets encountered the Japanese ships as they came into the Leyte Gulf and picked them off in separate pieces. It was one of the largest naval engagements in history and a disaster for the Japanese. They lost four aircraft carriers and 24 other fighting ships, while their opponents lost one light carrier and five other vessels.

The Gulf of Leyte was the first time the Japanese made concerted use of a new form of warfare—kamikaze attacks. Pilots flying planes loaded with explosives and fuel made suicide attacks on Allied ships, using their planes as massive munitions. Such desperate tactics became a regular feature of the war from then on, young men sacrificing their lives piloting kamikaze boats and planes in defense of the homeland.

In January, the Allies landed on Luzon, the most important of the Philippine islands. With the Japanese fleet so badly mauled, there was little prospect of support or rescue for the Japanese troops there. They fought on not in hopes of victory but with the intention of holding up the enemy for as long as possible. When the city of Manila fell at the end of January, troops took to the hills, where they fought on until June.

On the Asian mainland, the Japanese spent the first half of 1944 on the offensive, with attacks in China and India.

The attack on British-controlled India came first. Following a diversionary attack in February, the main offensive began in early March. But the diversion was defeated too quickly, freeing up British and Indian forces to tackle the main thrust. The Japanese were halted and then driven back at Imphal and Kohima. Supply lines failed and disease began to take its toll. By June, the Japanese forces were in retreat, many soldiers refusing to obey orders for a counter-attack. At the start of July, the offensive was called off.

Operation Ichi-Go, the offensive against China, was more of a success. The Chinese forces were not as well trained, led, or organized as those of their allies, despite support and training from the British and Americans. Over the course of eight months, the Japanese significantly increased their holdings in China. The aim was not just to take territory from the Chinese, but also to deprive the Americans of airfields in China from which they were bombing the Japanese. In this regard, it was a limited success as there was disruption but the Americans found other bases of operations. In taking territory, it was something of a self-defeating victory. The Japanese took control of cities but could not control the countryside around them. Their troops ended up spread thin to govern what they had taken. And while it was a significant blow for the Chinese nationalists under Chiang Kai-Shek, it did little to impede the advance of the Western Allies.

The defeat of the Japanese invasion of India opened the way for fresh Allied attacks into Burma. They drove back the broken Japanese forces then followed them into the occupied territory in late 1944.

Early in 1945, the Allies began a series of amphibious landings. Targeting territory further south in Burma, they took control of islands and peninsulas, inflicting a series of defeats and some heavy casualties on the Japanese. In the north, ongoing offensives achieved progress despite the withdrawal of some Chinese troops to counter the Ichi-Go offensive.

By early 1945, the Japanese were being pushed back everywhere except mainland China. For them, the war was not yet lost, but there was no visible way that it could be won.

Chapter 12 – The Invasion of Italy

Though Germany and Japan were both under pressure from the middle of 1943, neither was the first part of the Axis to give way. That honor would go to the oldest of Europe's far right regimes and the weak link in the chain of Hitler's ambitions—Fascist Italy.

With Africa taken, Churchill proposed that the Anglo-American forces there move on to attack the "soft underbelly" of Axis Europe. The Italians had shown in both Africa and the Balkans that they were not as formidable militarily as their German comrades. A landing in Italy was likely to be easier than almost anywhere else in Europe, despite the presence of German forces sent to reinforce the Italians. Supply routes could be maintained thanks to Allied control of Malta and North Africa. And from Italy, the Allies could march north into the heart of Hitler's empire.

The American focus was still on a direct assault into northern Europe. But the British persuaded them to accept a compromise strategy. A smaller invasion of Italy in 1943 would keep the Mediterranean war going, while the bulk of Allied forces prepared to invade France the following year.

The first step in the invasion of Italy was to take the island of Sicily. This began on July 10, 1943, when paratroopers and seaborne forces landed on the island. It was a joint Anglo-American operation, with the Americans led by Patton and the British by Montgomery. The two men's dislike of each other fueled a rivalry that helped to drive them on but did little for cooperation between the Allies.

The main advance toward Messina was meant to be made by the British. When they were held up by Italian and German troops, Patton took the opportunity to increase the Americans' role. Through advances north and then east, he reached Messina before the British.

The Axis forces evacuated the island, leaving it in Allied hands in the middle of August. The fighting had lasted just over a month, during which time the Allies had gained further valuable experience of amphibious and airborne assaults.

Meanwhile, Mussolini's political position was crumbling beneath his feet. Seeing that an Allied invasion of Italy was likely, he had begged Hitler to make peace with the USSR and send his troops west to face the threat. Hitler refused.

The invasion of Sicily further undermined Mussolini's position. Hitler summoned him to a humiliating meeting on July 19. On the same day, an Allied bombing raid hit Rome for the first time, highlighting Italy's newfound vulnerability.

Within the Italian leadership, Mussolini's friends were turning against him. His Fascist colleagues called upon King Victor Emmanuel III to retake the constitutional powers that had been taken by Mussolini. On July 25, the king replaced Mussolini with Marshal Badoglio and had the former dictator arrested.

When this news got out, many Italians celebrated, believing that the war was over. But it wouldn't be that easy. Badoglio maintained the pretense of loyalty to Germany, even as he negotiated a peace with the Allies. Despite his protests, German troops moved into the country, ready to deal with a potential Italian defection. An armistice agreement with the Allies was signed by Badoglio's representatives on September 3 but kept secret for several days.

On the same day that the armistice was signed, Allied troops crossed the Strait of Messina and landed in mainland Italy. They faced little opposition. The Italians were in disarray, many unopposed to the arrival of the British and Americans. The Germans correctly believed that this was not the main invasion force and so held back.

On September 8, the armistice signed by Badoglio's government was made public. Italy was surrendering to the Allies. The Germans had been preparing for this possibility. Within minutes of the official announcement, they launched Operation Achse. Italian troops across Europe were contained and disarmed by the Germans. In Italy, the Germans seized control of the north of the country, effectively turning it into another occupied territory. In the south, forces commanded by Kesselring continued their tactics of slow retreat and resistance to the Allies.

On the 9th, the Allies launched their main invasion. At Taranto, British troops landed with relatively little difficulty. At Salerno, the Americans faced stiff opposition from the

Germans, who at first managed to contain them within a limited beachhead on the coast. But German efforts were hampered by the need to manage the Italians. The Allied troops, many of them veterans of the North African campaign, began to advance up the peninsula.

Meanwhile, Hitler was making moves to keep political control of Italy. Schemes were hatched to kidnap the king and government, but these came to nothing. The one success came in the rescue of Mussolini. The former dictator was due to be handed over to the Allies as part of Italy's surrender, and he was being moved around to keep him out of German hands. But on September 12, a daring raid by German commandos took him out of Italian hands and into those of the Nazis.

To call it a rescue would be to overstate Mussolini's degree of freedom after the raid. He went from being a captive of his fellow countrymen to a relatively comfortable captive of the Germans. He was used as a puppet leader for the Italian Social Republic, as the Germans had labeled the part of Italy they occupied. He was a symbol that allowed them to add legitimacy to that occupation.

As the Allies advanced toward Rome, they faced an increasingly difficult campaign. Mountainous terrain divided by rivers made for a challenging advance. Field Marshal Kesselring had convinced Hitler that the Germans should defend southern Italy, keeping Allied air power as far from Germany as possible for as long as possible. This also bought time to prepare defensive lines further north.

A German defensive line south of Rome held the Allies up for months over the winter of 1943-4. American, British,

Canadian, French, and Polish troops were all brought into action in a series of offensives aimed at breaking through a narrow part of the front close to Monte Cassino. At last, in May 1944, they did it. An opportunity was missed to trap the German 10th Army as it retreated, but the symbolically important city of Rome was occupied without a fight on June 4.

The Allied invasion of France a few days later led to a change in the Allied forces in Italy. Experienced units were withdrawn ready for operations to take southern France. Other troops were sent to replace them, including some from Brazil, which had joined the Allied side in 1942. But these could not entirely make up for the loss of veteran soldiers.

In August 1944, the Allies began another substantial offensive in Italy. They made progress, but not as much as Churchill wanted. This was not the decisive victory he sought, one which would let them get into Eastern Europe before the Soviets and help set the stage for the new post-war order.

Partisan activity was on the rise. Resistance groups, many of them motivated by left-wing politics, took up arms against the Germans in the north and in the border region between Allied and Axis Italy. As other Italians fought on for the Germans, the fight for Italy took on an element of civil war.

By early 1945, winter weather, combined with the need to withdraw troops to other fronts, brought the Allied advance to a temporary halt. Italy lay divided, as did the attention of the Western Allies. The eyes of the world were now on France.

Chapter 13 – From D-Day to the Bulge

While it is unfair on the soldiers who fought in Italy that their campaign is not better remembered, it is also unsurprising. It was overshadowed by another operation carried out by the Western Allies, one so bold and so ingenious that it remains one of the most amazing accomplishments in the history of warfare.

This was Operation Overlord.

The Germans were expecting the Allied invasion of Western Europe to come through northern France. It was a logical option, given the short distance across the Channel from England. They therefore prepared for such an invasion, building up the defensive system known as the Atlantic Wall. Obstacles were placed on beaches. Concrete fortifications were built all along the coast. Artillery was put into place and troops stationed to repel the attack.

The Allies made extensive preparations of their own. From July 1943 onwards, they began training and practicing for the invasion, which would consist of an amphibious assault combined with airborne landings and supported by bombardments by sea and air. Massive floating components for harbors were constructed, so that they could follow the troops across the Channel and allow supplies to be unloaded. These Mulberry harbors meant that the Allies didn't have to start by seizing a port.

The Allies also began a massive campaign of deception to trick the Germans into expecting the main attack to come around the French port of Calais. The German agents the British had turned at the start of the war fed misinformation to their handlers. The First US Army Group was created, a non-existent force supposedly based in south-east England. Set and prop makers from the theaters of London were brought out to mock up an army camp, radio signals were sent out just to be intercepted, and General Patton, taken out of real command for mistreatment of soldiers in Italy, was put in charge to convince the Germans that the army was a real threat.

The invasion was launched on June 6, 1944. The night before, signals went out to the French resistance to sabotage German communication and transport systems. Just after midnight, 24,000 paratroopers were dropped. As dawn approached, an armada sailed across the Channel from England.

It was the largest amphibious invasion in history. Over 4,000 ships, barges, and landing craft were used to deposit 133,000 soldiers onto five stretches of the Norman coast. Two of the beaches were taken by the Americans, two by the British, and one by the Canadians.

These landings took place in the face of German forces and many men died before even making it off the beaches. Casualties were at their highest for the Americans on

Omaha Beach, where they became trapped beneath high cliffs.

Months of preparation paid off. Though the Allies didn't take their objectives on the first day, they all managed to establish holds on the French coast. While Hitler held back forces to face the invasion he still expected at Calais, the Allies began fighting their way inland.

On June 12, the Allies linked up their five bridgeheads. They held a stretch of land 60 miles long and up to 15 miles in depth, but major objectives, including the town of Caen, remained in German hands.

The problem for the Allies was the Norman countryside. With its narrow, winding roads between tall hedgerows, it gave the advantage to the defenders, who had plenty of places to lie in ambush. The Allies also struggled to overcome stiff German resistance in key places. It took until July 21 to completely take Caen, by which time the town was in ruins.

On the other hand, troops and supplies were pouring in. The Mulberry harbors were a success. Though one was destroyed in a storm on June 19, the other was repaired and remained operational. Over the next ten months, it would be used to unload 2.5 million men and 4 million tons of supplies.

Among the German high command, there was a growing realization that the war could not be won and that Hitler could not be reasoned with. On July 20, a group of German officers and politicians tried to assassinate him with a bomb, so that they could take over and make peace with the Allies. They failed. Hitler purged the upper echelons of the German army. Rommel, the hero of Africa, was among those who took their own lives rather than face trial and execution.

The Allies were making advances, but the Germans still had them contained in north-west France. A breakthrough was needed.

That breakthrough came with Operation Cobra. Launched on July 25, this was a concerted effort by the Americans to apply huge pressure against the Germans in a single sector. Once the enemy lines had been weakened, the US Third Army, led by a reinstated Patton, punched through and headed out across France.

This was the Allies turning the German's own tactics against them, a fast-moving column of armored troops creating a hole in the enemy lines, then launching an aggressive campaign that left the defenders without time to recover. It was an attack of which Guderian or Rommel would have been proud.

Between Patton's breakthrough and advances elsewhere along the lines, a substantial portion of the German forces became surrounded at Falaise. The Germans rushed to get out of the trap while the Allies hurried to complete their encirclement. Though many Germans escaped, 50,000 were captured.

Falaise showed that the rifts at the top of the Allied hierarchy were still not healed, as Patton blamed Montgomery for the failure to close the gap sooner and so capture more Germans.

Patton's breakout and the fall of the Falaise pocket signaled the end of any hopes the Axis forces had of containing the Allies. Allied troops made broad advances across France, while their opponents, ordered to hold every inch of ground by Hitler, were forced into a fighting retreat.

In Germany, hasty preparations were being made to defend the homeland. The Siegfried Line, a system of defenses along the border with France, had been abandoned as unnecessary in 1940. Now, rusted padlocks were removed from bunkers and empty stores were resupplied as troops arrived. Attacking the Siegfried Line would cost the Allies dearly in blood and time, but like the Maginot Line before it, it would not be enough to hold back invasion.

In Paris, the French Resistance rose up against the Germans on August 19. American and French troops rushed to aid the city as the Germans threatened to destroy it. They arrived on the 24th and on the 25th the French capital was liberated. It was a moment of huge symbolic importance, but the war for France was still ongoing.

On September 17, Allied forces under Montgomery made a bold attempt to smash through German positions in the Netherlands and strike into Germany. Operation Market Garden involved paratroop landings at a string of bridges that led deep into enemy-held territory. A swift armored advance would then break through the German lines and link up with the paratroopers, creating a route for Allied forces to outflank the Germans and cross the Rhine into Germany.

Market Garden was an over-ambitious failure. The advance could not reach the paratroopers quickly enough. Those at the end of the line of advance were left isolated for days, fending off German attacks. They eventually had to withdraw.

The failure of Market Garden added to tensions within the Allied high command. But the Allies, unlike the Germans, had the ability to productively discuss differences, vent some of their frustrations, and let dissenting voices be heard. On the Axis side, the autocratic Hitler was unwilling to listen to those who disagreed with him, men who often understood military matters better than he did. Disagreements were suppressed and men walked on eggshells around their leader.

On December 16, Hitler launched a counter-attack. Once again moving through the relatively undefended Ardennes forest, Panzer forces aimed to break through the Allied lines at a weak point. To support this, German commandos infiltrated the Allied forces, disguising themselves as officers so that they could spread confusion among the troops. German paratroops landed behind the Allied lines so that, as in the Market Garden plan, they could hold key positions along the route to aid the advance of tanks and infantry.

This second Ardennes offensive seemed to start well. The Allies were caught by surprise and the Germans made substantial advances.

But the possibility of success was illusory. The Germans had far fewer tanks and soldiers available than in 1940, while the Allies had more men with more experience. The infiltration work had little impact, the German agents being quickly caught. As the advance slowed and then ground to a halt, the paratroopers were left isolated behind enemy lines, forced to scatter and in many cases surrender.

The failed offensive became the Battle of the Bulge, as it created a bulge in the Allied lines but not a breakthrough. The Allied advance on Germany was delayed by over a month. But that month had cost Hitler his last substantial reserves. He would never again be able to launch a counter-attack.

There was no stopping the Allied advance.

Chapter 14 – The Fall of Germany

By the beginning of 1945, Germany effectively stood alone in Europe. Though German troops still occupied large chunks of several countries, Germany's principle ally, Italy, was at war with itself. Units from other countries, including anti-Soviet partisans from various parts of Eastern Europe, still fought on the Axis side, but they all did so under German military leadership.

In the west, the Allies made steady advances into Germany itself. The British and Canadians led the charge in the north, while in the south the Americans bore the brunt of the fighting. There, the focus was on demolishing Germany's industrial might in the Ruhr region. The fall of industrial cities such as Metz deprived the Germans of the ability to produce the materials of war.

Even during the last year of the war, the Germans were proving how advanced their military technology was. Following the D-Day landings, V-1 and V-2 rockets had been launched against British cities. German jet planes joined propeller-driven aircraft in the skies above Germany, though such superior technology, deployed in small numbers, was insignificant in the overall balance of the war.

As they advanced, there were again divisions behind the scenes between the Western Allies. Churchill was eager to push forward as far as possible, to occupy land before the Soviets could, as he believed that they would not let go of any territory they took. Eisenhower was more cautious, concerned with the possibility of over-stretching in the face of the Germans. In particular, he was wary of rumors of the German Alpine Redoubt.

The Alpine Redoubt was one of two important rumors floating around the German military at the time, both untrue but both important in shaping the final months of the war.

The Alpine Redoubt was a supposed plan for German troops to set up a fortified zone in the Alps. This would become a last place of resistance, where they could hold out for a long time against the Allies. In reality, such a plan had been rejected by Hitler earlier in the war, and by the time he considered the possibility it was too late. There was no redoubt.

The other rumor, encouraged by German propagandists, was that the sides were about to change. Many Germans believed, as Churchill did, that a confrontation between the Soviets and the west was inevitable. Some believed that it would come when the Allied forces of east and west met in Germany. At that point, the more optimistic German commanders insisted, the Allies would stop fighting the remaining Germans and side with them against the menace of communism. Some German commanders tried to reach out to the Allies and make this a reality. But for all the concerns about Stalin in the west, even Churchill never considered such a plan. His priority, and that of all the Allied commanders, was putting down the German menace once and for all.

On the Eastern Front, the Soviets continued to advance through territories occupied by the Germans. They took Silesia and Pomerania and advanced into Austria, taking Vienna. In the Balkans, the Yugoslav communist resistance under Tito had become a force to be reckoned with. German troops in Yugoslavia and the locals who had sided with them looked increasingly isolated and vulnerable.

In Italy, the Allies launched their last major offensive in April 1945. As the Allied troops advanced, Italian partisans declared a general uprising. The war became a swirling mess of movement. German troops fought rearguard actions, buying time for others to retreat. In places, Allied forces got behind them, cutting off their routes of retreat.

Meanwhile, secret negotiations were underway between representatives of the German and Allied commanders in Italy. Despite Hitler's orders, the Germans were looking for a peaceful way out. These negotiations faltered at times, as the military and political situation changed, but they laid the groundwork for the end of the fighting.

Among those fleeing the battlefront was Mussolini. On April 27, his convoy was captured by partisans near Lake Como. He, his mistress, and several members of his cabinet were taken into captivity. The next day, they were shot. In an act of degradation meant as vengeance for the treatment of partisans, their bodies were strung up in Milan, where people mocked and abused the corpses. In Italy, as elsewhere in Europe, many people were bitter at the way they had been treated by Axis regimes. As the Axis fell, that bitterness spilled out.

In Germany, Hitler took desperate measures to defend his crumbling empire. Youths, old men, and those previously excluded on health grounds were called up for military service. There was little time to train or prepare them. They were given weapons and thrust into the lines, ready to fight off the advancing Allies.

Civil society was shut down to provide personnel for the military. The only parts of universities still teaching were the medical schools. Only textbooks and Hitler's books were published. Theatres and music halls closed. Even military personnel saw their lives changed, as men were stripped from the navy to bolster the army. There was no point continuing the fight at sea if the homeland was lost.

On the Eastern Front, the forces pinned against the Baltic were finally forced to surrender in the face of overwhelming Soviet might. Meanwhile, senior Nazi officials were fleeing west, often taking their close associates and wealth with them.

Earlier in the war, Hitler had moved between a number of custom-built bases around Europe. Now he hunkered down in a bunker beneath Berlin, the capital of the empire that he had thought would last for a thousand years. His behavior was increasingly erratic, his view of the situation increasingly detached from reality. He could not conceive of the possibility that Germany might lose the war. Military units were reorganized and renamed in a desperate attempt to maintain the illusion of a potent fighting force. Command positions were reshuffled as men disappointed him through their failures or through disagreeing with his views. One of his few sensible decisions was giving Kesselring independent authority in the south if the German empire should be split in two.

The Soviets were the first to reach Berlin. On April 16, they began their assault on the city. For political reasons, Stalin let two different field marshals, each with their own army and their own plan, attack the German capital.

The fighting for Berlin was as bitter as any in the war. The Germans clung on with the desperation of the lost. Some hoped to hold off the Soviets long enough for the British and Americans to arrive, saving them from the feared Red Army. Others were so thoroughly indoctrinated with Nazi ideas that they could not consider the possibility of defeat. They fought street by street, combat sometimes breaking out next to the bread lines where starving civilians queued for food.

On April 30, Soviet troops stormed the Reichstag, the official seat of German government, and flew their red victory flag above the building. It was a powerful symbolic moment, marking the ascendancy of the Soviets in the east. But on the same day, a far more important event took place in the bunker.

Hitler had reached the end of the road. Seeing that he could not win, he committed suicide alongside his wife. Rather than have his body suffer the same indignities as Mussolini's corpse, he ordered that it be burnt outside the bunker. Petrol was in short supply, but his remaining subordinates did their best, cremating their leader in the pauses between the shellfire being rained down by Soviet artillery.

With Hitler gone, surrender became an option. Forces in Italy had already surrendered on the 29th. On May 7, Germany signed an unconditional surrender to the Allies. Troops in Prague fought on against the Soviets until the 11th and many elsewhere fled to western areas before surrendering.

The battle for Europe was over, but the war raged on.

Chapter 15 – The Fall of Japan

With the Japanese in retreat, the Allies began looking ahead to the invasion of Japan. As part of their preparations, they launched increasingly intense bombing campaigns against the Japanese mainland.

The problem for these bombers was the distance involved— a round trip of 3,000 miles from Saipan to the Japanese targets. A closer base would let them carry out more raids and there was a natural choice for that base. Iwo Jima, an island 760 miles from southeast Japan, was currently a base for Japanese fighters and the radar directing them against incoming attacks. Taking it would deprive the Japanese of an important defensive position as well as bringing Allied air power forward.

After days of bombardment, US troops landed on Iwo Jima in mid-February 1945. As on many of the Japanese-occupied islands, they made the landing relatively easily but became tied down in the face of protracted Japanese resistance. It took over a month to clear the island, during which time the Americans took heavy casualties and created one of the most iconic images of the war, a photograph of the raising of the stars and stripes over Mount Suribachi.

While the Marines fought for Iwo Jima, the US Air Force was changing its approach to bombing. On March 9, they switched from daytime high-altitude raids to nighttime firebombing, using napalm against Japanese cities made largely out of wood. In that first raid, 25% of Tokyo was destroyed and 80,000 people died. Based on these results, the planners concluded that they might be able to beat Japan without risking an invasion. Firebombing was extended to other major cities, burning the urban heart out of Japan.

Though the Allies were moving away from a focus on invading Japan, they still planned for it. The next step in the island-hopping approach was Okinawa. It had a garrison of 120,000 men, 10,000 aircraft, and a naval task force including the largest battleship ever built, the *Yamato*. This would be a hard fight.

Months of air raids and weeks of naval bombardment softened up Okinawa ready for the invasion. On April 1, the Americans made an unopposed landing on the island. This was followed by another grueling campaign to take out the dug-in defenders, which lasted until the end of June. During that time, hundreds of kamikaze pilots attacked the Allied fleet, sinking over a dozen destroyers. But the Japanese fleet also suffered, with the *Yamato* among the vessels sunk by American bombers.

While the Americans fought for Okinawa, the Australians were retaking Borneo. It was an equally protracted campaign that ended at the start of July with the collapse of Japanese defenses at Balikpapan.

In Burma, the Allies continued their offensive. The focus was on taking Rangoon, to gain control of this vital port and so ensure supply lines before the monsoon rains began. As Burmese forces rebelled against the Japanese, the Allies rushed forward by land and then launched a seaborne operation. They managed to take vital positions at Rangoon hours before the monsoon rains began.

The Japanese retreated through Burma. Their attempts at a counter-attack were thwarted and they lost thousands of men trying to break out of the country.

The Allied victory in Burma helped to secure the Ledo Road, a vital supply route for the Chinese. As well as taking part in operations in Burma, Chinese Nationalist armies launched spring offensives to retake large portions of their own land, including Hunan and Guangxi. The Chinese army, aided by the Allies, was better armed and trained than at any previous point in the war. While the country was still riven by internal strife, it had gained the ability to effectively fight back, especially now that Japanese resources were being drained by the island war.

On every front, the Japanese were in retreat. A strict code of honor kept military men from accepting defeat, but that result was now inevitable. With Allied submarines preventing imports and bombers destroying cities, the country was being worn away and victory was impossible.

As in Germany a few months earlier, all that was left to be decided was the terms on which defeat took place. In July, following a meeting at Potsdam, the Allies demanded that the Japanese surrender unconditionally. The Japanese government refused.

Following the fall of Okinawa and the destruction of the Japanese fleet there, the route to the mainland lay open. With the war in Europe over, troops from there started heading to the Pacific, ready to form an army of invasion. But experience showed that this was likely to be a costly and protracted campaign, one that could cost hundreds of thousands of Allied lives.

Unknown to the world, the Allies had a trump card up their sleeve. Since 1942, American, British, and Canadian scientists had been working in secret on a new weapon. Under the code-name of the Manhattan Project, they had developed the first atomic bombs, weapons unparalleled in their devastating power.

Rather than lose lives invading Japan, President Truman chose to use this weapon to intimidate the enemy into surrender. On August 6, 1945, an atomic bomb was used for the first time. Dropped on the city of Hiroshima, this single bomb killed 70-80,000 people. Three days later, another bomb was dropped on Nagasaki, killing 35-40,000.

As many people were being killed by conventional bombs, but the devastating power of the atom bomb shook the world. As unsettling for the Japanese was a declaration of war by the Soviets, who invaded the Japanese puppet state of Manchuria on August 9. Despite the wider war, the USSR had not previously been fighting Japan. Now there was no hope that the Soviets would act as a moderating force for the Japanese in negotiations with the Allies.

On September 2, the Japanese surrendered unconditionally to General MacArthur on the USS *Missouri*.

The Second World War was over. The question now was what its consequences would be.

Chapter 16 – Aftermath

In Europe, a fresh war threatened to break out immediately, as Tito's Yugoslav forces tried to occupy parts of Austria. Swift maneuvers by the Western Allies cut off these ambitions, but there were concerns that Stalin might back Tito, giving him the confidence to fight. Fortunately, Stalin wasn't interested in supporting Yugoslav ambition. Tito's plans came to nothing.

Tito's behavior threatened to plunge the world back into war. But other revelations transformed people's understanding of the war and of what it meant to be human.

As Allied troops advanced across Europe, they discovered the Nazi concentration camps. Unknown to most people, Hitler's regime had been murdering Jews, gays, Slavs, dissidents, and others they saw as opponents. This wasn't just an occasional killing. It was the systematic murder of millions of innocent people, using buildings and machines designed just for this purpose.

It was the most horrifying act ever committed by humanity. The revelation of the torments inflicted in Japanese prison camps only added to a sense of collective horror. Entire fields of social psychology developed just to understand how this could happen. The international Jewish community, devastated by their losses, gained a renewed determination to found a safe, secure homeland of their own.

War crimes trials followed. The world came together in condemnation not only of the camps but of other murders carried out during the war. Senior Nazi officials were tried at Nuremberg. Ten men were hanged. One committed suicide to escape execution. Many more were imprisoned.

The process of recovery was about more than retribution. The Allies carried out a thorough program to remove Nazi influences from Germany and to help the country rebuild, so as not to leave an embittered nation seeking revenge, as it had after World War One. The United Nations was founded to create a place for nations to peacefully settle their differences, and so to avoid another war.

While the World War was over, the Cold War was just beginning. Churchill and a throng of senior Germans had been right—confrontation between the Soviet Union and the capitalist west was now inevitable. The question was how it would play out.

In the aftermath of the war, Europe was divided into two spheres of influence. In the east, the Soviets spread communist rule. In the west, the Americans, British, and French ensured the ascendancy of capitalist democracy. For decades, the two faced off against each other. The fear of global war and of atomic weapons, as demonstrated during the Second World War, kept them from direct conflict, even as they fought through proxy nations.

Outside of Europe, the Second World War marked the effective end of Europe's overseas empires. The Italians and Germans lost their colonies in the war. The British, Dutch, and French were left in no condition to reclaim those they had lost or to retain those now yearning for freedom. Over the following twenty years, their former colonies broke free, some peacefully and some by force.

Into their place stepped the USA, the ascendant global power. Having cast off isolationism and proved their power, the Americans were determined to use it. They became the leaders of the Western world, politically as well as economically. The Second World War had turned an introverted nation into a global powerhouse.

Conclusion

The Second World War was the most devastating conflict that the Earth had ever seen. To say that all the world took part would be an exaggeration. After all, much of Africa and nearly all of Latin America stayed out of the conflict. Even several European countries did not fight. But it was a conflict of such scale that the whole world was transformed.

The effects of the war linger to this day, from the horrifying memories of the prison camps to the unifying impact of the United Nations. As the generation that fought the war passes away, it is more important than ever that we remember what happened and why, so that such devastation should never happen again.

Part 2: D Day
A Captivating Guide to the Battle for Normandy

Introduction

D-Day, the Allied invasion of German-held Normandy, was one of the most extraordinary achievements not only of the Second World War but in the whole of military history. Millions of Allied personnel were involved in launching the greatest sea-borne invasion ever undertaken. Incredible acts of cunning and of courage ensured success in an operation that changed the face of the war, opening a vast new front. It led to the liberation of France and the defeat of Nazi Germany.

Why was this extraordinary operation launched? How was it done? And what happened in the aftermath?

Chapter 1 – Why D-Day?

The Second World War was a conflict unlike any other that had come before. During the First World War, a network of alliances had turned a war in the Balkans into one that engulfed all of Europe, but fighting in the rest of the world was limited. World War Two, on the other hand, brought together a long-standing war between Japan and China, German attempts to create a European empire, and battles for control of colonies across Africa and Asia. When Japanese ambitions brought America into the fighting in 1941, it became a single maelstrom of destruction that spanned the globe, involving every leading military power and dozens of other nations.

In Europe, the Axis powers of Germany and Italy were the aggressors at every turn. The Germans occupied vast swathes of eastern Europe, half of Scandinavia, and western Europe all the way to the Atlantic Ocean. The fall of France briefly left Britain as the only sovereign and unconquered nation in Europe still opposing this tide of blood. The British, aided by their colonies, allies in the Commonwealth, and thousands of soldiers who had fled the conquered countries, fought on in the skies above Europe and in colonial possessions around the world, especially North Africa, where fighting swayed back and forth from early in the war.

It was the arrival of the Americans that turned the tide of that campaign. Though it was a Japanese attack that brought them into the war, from the start, they made Europe their main priority. They believed it would be easier to defeat Germany first and then its ally Japan.

The Americans joined the British in North Africa late in 1942, bringing their substantial economic resources and a vast pool of manpower to bear. Though the campaign had its setbacks, it signaled the near-inevitable defeat of the Axis powers in the face of superior resources. The Allies drove the Axis forces back into a smaller and smaller pocket in north-east Tunisia until the last Germans and Italians were forced to surrender.

North Africa was important for the control of supply routes, but it was also a springboard for an invasion of Europe. Behind the scenes, the British and Americans continued to argue about how to knock out Germany, the leader of their European opponents and the most powerful enemy in that theatre of the war. The Americans favored developing a grand plan to invade France, liberating another potentially powerful ally, and push from there directly into Germany. The British, who had fewer resources and struggled from the start with the strength of the German military, favored a more cautious approach, fighting step-by-step, taking opportunities as they came. If they could win the war by bombing Germany or invading through some other route, they could avoid the costs and risks of a sea-borne landing in France.

The result was a compromise. Some resources were put into invading Italy from Africa in 1943, while a larger portion were held in reserve to invade France the following year.

The Italian campaign was a success, as that country's government almost immediately flipped sides, forcing the Germans and those Italians who backed them to fight against local resistance as well as foreign invaders. But it was a slow-burning campaign in which Kesselring, the German commander, built a series of defensive lines that slowed down and eventually halted the Allied advance.

Meanwhile, the war was turning against the Germans in Eastern Europe. Having betrayed and invaded their former allies in the Soviet Union, the Germans became bogged down in a grueling war against a nation of immense resources and unquenchable determination. The Eastern Front became a huge drain on the German war machine, making a successful invasion in the west more plausible.

Russia's presence on the Allied side also weakened Britain's attempts to restrain the Americans. The British wanted to hold back from invading France for as long as possible, letting the Russians wear down the Axis. But the Russians naturally wanted to see the pressure on them relieved by western intervention sooner rather than later. It was a testament to the political skill of Prime Minister Winston Churchill and his diplomats that the British had restrained their Atlantic allies as long as they had. But with two parts of their tripartite alliance calling for a new front, and with Britain's drained resources making the nation less influential within that alliance, it was time to give in to the inevitable.

There was another factor playing on the minds of the American and British planners, beyond balancing American boldness with British pragmatism. That was the future of post-war Europe. The alliance with Russia, while vital to victory, was an uneasy one. The governments of the western nations feared the spread of communism and the potential for Russian hegemony over large swathes of Europe. As the Russians gained momentum, and German defeat in the east became inevitable, the question wasn't whether the Russians would occupy parts of Europe when the war ended, it was how large those parts would be. The longer the Americans and British left it before opening up a new western front, the more of Europe would be dominated by communism in the aftermath. Outmaneuvering the Soviets wasn't as urgent a priority as defeating the Nazis, but it was important, especially to the belligerently anti-communist Churchill.

And so, the planning began for Operation Overlord, the Allied invasion of France. Over the winter of 1943-44, other options were gradually abandoned. Even an American scheme for a simultaneous landing in southern France was set aside, thanks to pressure from the British. The full weight of the available Allied resources in the west would be poured into this single operation. It would be carried out by a mixed force, predominantly American, British, and Canadian, but also featuring armies in exile from nations such as France and Poland.

While the details of the plan were a carefully guarded secret, the Germans knew that the Allies were going to invade. The question was where and when.

And so, on both sides of the Channel, forces were prepared for one of the most daring and decisive battles in history.

D-Day was coming.

Chapter 2 – Preparation

Among the first steps in preparing for D-Day was selecting the men who would lead the operations and creating a leadership structure for the combined military force. This was not a simple matter of selecting the most senior or most skilled officers. The operation would be led by a mixture of American and British men, many of whom were proud of their own national armies and reticent about working under foreigners. Operations in North Africa had shown that the historic experience of the British armed forces and the youthful power of the Americans led to two different flavors of arrogance that could clash at every level, from arguments in high command meetings to fist fights in infantry canteens. Pride, politics, and personalities all came into play.

The result was the selection of the American Dwight D. Eisenhower as overall commander for Operation Overlord. The diplomatic Eisenhower was popular with the American leadership, liked by Churchill, and through his leadership in Africa had proved he could manage the tensions between the forces of these two great powers.

The leadership of the initial stages of Overlord, beginning with the D-Day landings, went to the British General Bernard Montgomery, who was also commander of the ground forces. Because of their experience, British officers held many other senior posts, leading to tensions that Eisenhower had to balance. His job was made more challenging by senior air officers on both the American and British sides, who constantly resisted attempts to assert authority over them and to put military effort into an invasion. They believed their bombing campaigns could win the war and the plans for Overlord were a waste of effort.

Even before Eisenhower was in place, another important part of the preparation was underway – intelligence gathering. Early in the war, Britain had turned around its neglected military intelligence operation to become possibly the best intelligence gathering organization in the world. Now that apparatus was tasked with preparing for the invasion of France. Aerial reconnaissance flights began building up a picture of German forces and defenses in France, as well as the geography of the land they held. Holiday photographs of the French coast were collected from ordinary Britons, adding to the picture. German military signals were intercepted and decoded, including those from the high-level Enigma machines, secretly decrypted through the work of Polish and British experts. The French resistance fed what information they could into the mix, using contacts established by British special operatives earlier in the war.

Intelligence gathering continued right up to the invasion itself. Everything from supply orders to visits by senior

German commanders gave the Allies information about the enemy forces.

Using this information, senior Allied commanders began planning for the campaign.

The biggest decision was where to land. They knew they were aiming for the coast of northern France, but where? Four major factors affected this choice: the distance across the English Channel to the site; how many men the beaches could hold; how heavily they were defended; and how far Allied air cover could reach to support the invasion.

The Pas de Calais was the closest landing ground and favored by some commanders for that reason. It held the major harbors of Calais, Boulogne, and Dunkirk, which could be used to unload troops and supplies. But that made it an obvious and heavily defended target, and a failed raid on Dieppe in 1942 had taught the British how costly such an attack could be. Brittany was too far away for a landing ground, so was quickly ruled out. A landing in the Cotentin Peninsula could too easily be contained by the Germans, preventing the Allies from breaking out of their initial bridgeheads.

Having eliminated most possibilities, the planners settled on the Calvados coast of Normandy. It was relatively poorly defended and had a series of broad beaches that would make excellent landing grounds. Having identified their target, the planners began outlining how they would take it.

American military planners had been working on this since 1942, but inevitably, there were arguments among the Allies. The phase line, which showed where American forces were expected to reach in the first 90 days, was removed from a map as the Americans did not want to commit to Montgomery's targets. It was a relatively minor issue, a line used to assess what supplies would be needed. But it took on symbolic significance as the big day approached and tensions rose.

The Allies could not wait until the plan was complete before assembling the forces that would carry it out. And so, in the spring of 1944, southern England became home to a vast assembly of armed forces, vehicles, and supplies. Hundreds of thousands of troops from across Europe and the English-speaking world gathered in previously quiet parts of the rural countryside. Alongside the Americans, British, and Canadians, there were Czechs, Frenchmen, Hungarians, Poles, and Jews from Austria and Germany. Almost every week, more Americans arrived. They all needed space to camp and to train, as well as supplies... With their chocolate and chewing gum, ordinary American infantrymen lived a life that seemed fantastically decadent compared with that of the war-weary and heavily rationed British.

In harbors along the south coast, 138 battleships, cruisers, and destroyers were mustered, along with 27 escorts, 2 submarines, 310 landing ships, and over 3,800 barges and landing craft. Together with minesweepers, motorboats, and supply ships, it was an incredible armada.

The troops didn't sit idly while they waited for the attack. Twenty-five miles of Devon countryside were cleared of its population for live-fire training exercises. Twelve-day courses prepared logistics officers for the complexities of supplying the invasion force. Maps of the real terrain were used for training, but with the names of places changed to maintain secrecy about where the landings were coming. Montgomery pushed the men hard to get them ready.

Hindsight would reveal gaps in this training. American troops rehearsed on the southern moors, the British on the flatlands of East Anglia. This terrain bore little similarity to the broken ground of the Norman Bocage, where winding roads, hills, and hedgerows provided plentiful cover and ambush points for defensive forces. The tactics practiced were generally those of the open order advance, rather than the infiltration tactics at which the Germans were skilled. But for all its limitations, a phenomenal amount was achieved in those months before the invasion.

Meanwhile, the less glamorous but no less vital work of logistics officers made the invasion possible. Ammunition, rations, vehicles, and medical supplies flowed across the Atlantic and into warehouses. Everything from biscuits to blood plasma was gathered and stored. Plans were made for how to distribute all these supplies to a huge army on the move through the fiercely contested territory.

The Mulberry harbors are the most famous part of this supply chain. Two prefabricated concrete harbors, they were built in large sections which could be towed across the Channel and then set in place at occupied beaches. This allowed men and supplies to be unloaded in places that had no port facility. It was thanks to this ingenious feat of engineering that the Allies could surprise the Germans by landing in an area without ports.

Alongside the supply ships, other communication and supply lines were prepared. The Petroleum Line Under The

Ocean (PLUTO) was laid down once the Allies were established in Normandy, allowing fuel to be pumped from England to France. Telephone cables were also prepared, ready to be laid beneath the Channel, securely connecting commanders in France with those in London.

In the weeks and months leading up to the invasion, the Allies softened up the Germans for the attack. Much of this was targeted at infrastructure rather than directly tackling military targets. Attacks by Allied bombers and by the French Resistance weakened communication and supply networks in northern France, to prevent the Axis powers from bringing their strength to bear against the invasion. 1,500 of the 2,000 locomotives available in the region were taken out of action. Bridges across the Seine and the Loire were destroyed. Railway junctions and radar stations were also sabotaged. These attacks could not just be concentrated in the area around the invasion zone, as this would have given away the Allied plans, and so it took place across a broad area of northern France.

Ironically, the resistance of bomber commanders also helped pave the way for the attack. Reluctant to be diverted from their strategic bombing campaign against German cities, they contributed as little as they could get away with to direct preparations for D-Day. Meanwhile, the appearance of the American Mustang fighter to protect Allied bombers led to heavy losses among German aircraft, adding to Allied aerial superiority.

This bombing came at a cost. Twelve thousand Belgian and French civilians lost their lives – fewer than Churchill had expected, but still a tragic loss.

In the days leading up to the attack, preparations intensified. Minesweepers cleared the sea lanes for the invasion fleet. The Allies already had a tight hold on the Channel and had sunk half the U-boats trying to attack shipping in the region. The sea lanes were clear of German threats.

The original date for D-day – the launch date of the invasion – was 5 June 1944. Poor weather postponed it until the next day. And so, it was on the night of the fifth to the sixth of June the heaviest bombardment fell on the German defenders. As the fleet set out, 5,200 tons of bombs were dropped by heavy bombers on Axis defenses. As daylight came, medium bombers and fighters took over. Allied warships began pounding the German coastal emplacements.

Only now did the Germans begin to realize what they were up against. Achieving this surprise was an extraordinary part of the campaign. There were many more extraordinary acts to come.

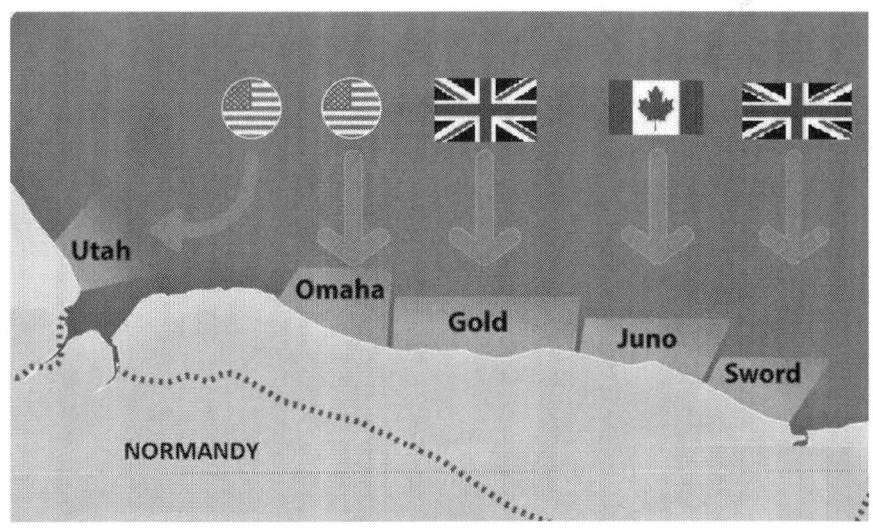

D Day attack plan. The five arrows are pointing to code names for five sectors of the allied invasion. These names are Utah, Omaha, Gold, Juno and Sword and will be discussed in greater detail later in the book.

Chapter 3 – Deception

In preparation for Operation Overlord, massive and ingenious deception operations were used to trick the Germans into believing the attack would not come in Normandy. Even after the attack began, these preparations would trick them into thinking it was a feint. Under the overall heading of Operation Bodyguard, several different plans, most famously Operation Fortitude, were used to trick the Axis commanders.

The Allied efforts were widespread. In the Mediterranean, an actor who looked like Montgomery was dressed up as the general and used to create a story the invasion might occur there. Diplomatic pressure on neutral Sweden, together with a supposed invasion force in Scotland, created the illusion an attack might come in occupied Norway. But while such actions did a little to spread German resources and sow confusion, they were nothing compared with the focus on the Pas de Calais.

This web of lies was easy to weave because it was so believable. The Pas de Calais was the attack route that made the most sense, thanks to the short journey across the Channel and the presence of several substantial ports.

These facts made the lie easy to swallow, making it easier to deceive Hitler as to the Allies' true intentions.

Double agents were crucial to the success of this plan. Early in the war, the British tracked down every German agent in the country. Some were imprisoned, but others were turned, becoming British double agents. They were used to feed false information to Germany on several occasions. They provided a mixture of true and false information that made the lie of a Calais invasion convincing.

The most important double agent was a Spaniard named Juan Pujol Garcia, codenamed Garbo. The Germans were so convinced Garbo was a useful spy for them that Hitler awarded him the Iron Cross. Garbo fed the Germans information about the supposed Calais landing, which was scheduled after the real operation further to the west. After D-Day came, Garbo continued feeding false information to his contacts in Berlin, who continued to believe that the D-Day landings were not where the major invasion was going to take place. This subterfuge provided the Allied forces with extra time to consolidate their positions and press forward before the Germans committed any additional forces.

One of the most extraordinary parts of the plan was an imaginary invasion force, the First U.S. Army Group (FUSAG). FUSAG was created in 1943 as an administrative formation to help planning for the invasion and was initially led by General Omar Bradley. Bradley and his staff were moved to the headquarters of FUSAG, a force which existed only on paper.

FUSAG was notionally based in Kent, the natural staging ground for an army assembling to cross the Channel from Dover to Calais. Set-builders from film studios and theatres were brought from London to Kent, where they built a fictitious army. There were barracks and tents for the troops, and life-sized models of landing craft and tanks, all convincing enough to trick the limited aerial reconnaissance efforts of the Germans.

Radio signals were used to support the illusion. Military radio traffic filled the airwaves of Kent and was intercepted by German military intelligence as it drifted across the Channel. The Allies could tell this had been effective because they themselves were so much better at intercepting and decrypting German signals.

As the date of the invasion approached, a new leader was assigned to FUSAG. General George S. Patton was known for his aggressive and effective command style, which he had demonstrated against the Germans in North Africa. He had been removed from command in Italy due to disciplinary issues, and now he was put in charge of the imaginary FUSAG. The Germans rightly feared Patton. His arrival to command FUSAG therefore made it even more convincing and intimidating.

One of the most elaborate charades of the operation was used to bolster FUSAG. A badly injured Panzer officer, held in Britain as a POW, was being returned to Germany. He was told he would be travelling through Kent. There he saw armed forces being massed for an invasion and was introduced to Patton as commander of FUSAG. This provided the Germans with eyewitness testimony for the existence of the force in Kent.

What they didn't know was the POW had been diverted through Hampshire, where the real armies were assembling, and where Patton had been brought specifically for the encounter. The troops were the D-Day armies preparing to attack Normandy, and Patton was a visitor like the German prisoner. The whole thing was a lie.

The activities of the Allied air forces were adapted to match the rest of Operation Bodyguard. Prior to Montgomery taking over, the planners for the invasion had concentrated aerial reconnaissance flights on the Norman coast, where the attacks were scheduled to land. Montgomery and his staff quickly changed this, extending aerial reconnaissance to cover the whole Channel coast, focusing on the area around Calais. This increased the effort needed to gather useful information but ensured these flights would not provide the Germans with clues about where the attack was coming. Similarly, when they started bombing German communication lines in the build-up to the invasion, the air forces spread their effort over a wide area, maintaining the illusion the Allies were focused on the Pas de Calais.

All this effort would have been for nothing if German intelligence gathering had been more effective. But Allied efforts to counter it paid off. The turning and incarceration of spies at the start of the war ensured there were no German accurately reporting on events in Britain. Allied aerial superiority prevented effective German aerial reconnaissance, preventing the enemy seeing through the charade that was FUSAG.

The overall impact of this work was substantial. The Germans had to stretch their defenses to cover a great length of the French coast, preventing them from concentrating their resources where the invasion was going to fall. Hitler held the veteran Fifteenth Army around Calais for weeks after the invasion arrived, as he wanted them to fight off the strike by FUSAG.

Chapter 4 – The Commanders

Many extraordinary men led the Allied offensive on D-Day.

General Dwight D. Eisenhower

The man at the very top, Eisenhower was the supreme commander of the Allied Expeditionary Forces.

Born in Texas in 1890, Eisenhower was descended from German Mennonites, ironically a sect of extreme pacifists. He graduated from West Point in 1915 as an unexceptional new officer, coming in 61st academically and 125th for discipline out of a class of 164. He served in several posts before attending the Command and General Staff School, where he graduated first out of a class of 275, and then went on to the Army War College.

Eisenhower served in the Philippines as an aide to General MacArthur but left before the Japanese invasion in 1941. Back in the USA, he gained favor by planning the largest war games the country had ever run. When America joined the war, he was sent to join the planning team in Washington, where he was involved in early discussions about an invasion of Europe.

As overall commander of the Anglo-American invasions of North Africa, Sicily, and mainland Italy, Eisenhower had the experience for his role in Overlord. He lacked experience as a combat commander and was not an outstanding tactician. But he had the tact and political skill to manage the various strong personalities under his command, including Montgomery and Patton, as well as to delicately handle the French, who wanted to be treated as a major power despite their lack of military strength.

General Bernard Montgomery

Born in 1887, Montgomery went from school to the Royal Military College at Sandhurst. There he was demoted for setting fire to a fellow cadet and didn't graduate high enough to secure a coveted post in the British Indian Army.

Montgomery spent the First World War progressing through the ranks as an infantry officer and was severely wounded at the First Battle of Ypres. The horrifying losses he saw in Flanders made him determined never to use such senseless tactics. He concluded that serious life-long study was needed for military command, shaping his studious approach to leadership.

During the Fall of France in 1940, Montgomery led the 3rd Division in the vanguard of the British Expeditionary Force (BEF). Events there proved his skill as a leader, leading to senior positions despite his undiplomatic manner.

In August 1942, he was made commander of British forces in North Africa. He turned around the dispirited 8th Army and defeated Rommel at Alam Halfa and El Alamein, becoming a hero to the beleaguered British. When the Americans arrived, Montgomery's abrupt handling of them contributed to poor Anglo-American relations, giving Eisenhower his first experience managing Montgomery's awkward personality.

For Operation Overlord, Montgomery was commander of the ground forces and Commander-in-Chief during the initial invasion. His revision of the operational plans made Overlord the success it was and later earned him a promotion to Field Marshal. But his arrogance and his insistence all their successes were down to his own planning ensured that he would continue to antagonize colleagues throughout the war.

General Miles Dempsey

One of Montgomery's most trusted subordinates, Dempsey led a large part of the British and Canadian forces during the D-Day landings.

Born in 1896, Dempsey graduated from Sandhurst before becoming a British infantry officer in the First World War. Injured in a German gas attack, he had a lung removed. After the war, he served in posts around Europe and the British Empire, attended the Staff College, and continued his steady rise through the ranks.

As an infantry commander during the Fall of France, Dempsey led his men in several defensive battles. They played an important part in the rearguard during the retreat to Dunkirk.

Late in 1942, Dempsey was promoted to Lieutenant General and sent to join British forces in North Africa. There he caught the attention of Montgomery, becoming one of his most capable commanders. He helped plan the invasion of Sicily and commanded the airborne troops who spearheaded the attack.

Montgomery chose him to command the British Second Army, the main British and Canadian force, during the D-Day landings. Unlike his superior, Dempsey was modest and unassuming. Like Montgomery, he was an effective military commander.

Air Chief Marshal Sir Trafford Leigh-Mallory

Born in 1892, Leigh-Mallory was training to become a lawyer when the First World War broke out. He volunteered to join the British infantry as a private, quickly became a second lieutenant, and was put through officer training. After recovering from an injury, he joined the Royal Flying Corps, where he distinguished himself in the new field of aerial warfare.

Following the war, Leigh-Mallory stayed in the RAF. He received staff officer training and served in command, staff, and training posts.

In the late 1930s, Leigh-Mallory became commander of 12 Group, which he commanded during the Battle of Britain. An ambitious man, he was heavily involved in backroom politicking that was disruptive to the RAF. At times, he exaggerated the successes of his preferred tactics to further his career. His plotting paid off, and changes in the RAF saw him continue to rise through the ranks. He lobbied for a single overall commander to be created for Allied air operations during Overlord, and when this proposal was accepted, he was given the post.

Opinions of Leigh-Mallory varied. Montgomery liked him, as he provided the air support the general wanted. Eisenhower considered him capable but "somewhat ritualistic in outlook."

Admiral Sir Bertram Home Ramsay

Born in 1883, Ramsay joined the British Royal Navy in 1898. He quickly rose through the ranks and commanded several ships during the First World War.

Ramsay was brought back into service in 1939 by Churchill. Ramsay had retired in 1938. He oversaw Britain's naval defenses and in 1940 led Operation Dynamo, the evacuation from Dunkirk that brought home 338,000 Allied soldiers cut off by the advancing Germans.

Following Dunkirk, Ramsay grappled with the Germans for control of the Channel. He was involved in the invasions of Africa and Sicily, giving him the experience of seaborne landings.

Made Naval Commander-in-Chief for the D-Day landings, Ramsay coordinated a massive fleet of 7,000 vessels used to safely deliver 160,000 men onto the beaches on the first day.

Air Chief Marshal Sir Arthur Tedder

Born in Scotland in 1890, Tedder's early career was similar to Leigh-Mallory's. A civilian volunteer who joined the infantry at the start of World War One, he transferred to the Royal Flying Corps and stayed in the RAF after the war ended. He rose through the ranks, becoming Director General of Research at the Air Ministry in 1938.

Tedder was transferred to RAF Middle East Command in 1940. There, he provided air support for the evacuation of Crete and ground operations in North Africa. His tactical and administrative skills led to improvements in the British forces in Africa.

In 1943, Tedder took over Mediterranean Air Command. There he served under Eisenhower and took part in planning the invasions of Sicily and Italy. He came to Overlord with Eisenhower and served as Deputy Supreme Commander.

General Omar Bradley

Born in 1893, Bradley worked as a boiler maker before attending West Point in the same class as Eisenhower. Quiet and dependable, he rose through the ranks of the interwar American army, taking on command, training, and staff posts.

In 1942, Bradley oversaw the transformation of the U.S. 82nd Infantry Division into the first American airborne division. Graduating from West Point in the same class as Eisenhower, his classmates, and later his contemporaries, considered him quiet and dependable. He became the troubleshooter that helped to shape the Allied forces into a cohesive, fighting force. This was partly about building up the inexperienced American army, but it was also about keeping the peace between the Americans and British. He commanded II Corps in the last operations in Tunisia and in the invasion of Sicily.

As commander of the First United States Army (not to be confused with the fake First US Army Group), Bradley had overall command of the American ground forces during D-Day. Steady, capable, and discrete, he was excellent at reading a battlefield. Like Eisenhower, he helped to keep the peace in an operation sometimes troubled by strong personalities and the politicking prevalent in the air services.

Chapter 5 – The Men and Equipment

When looking at war, attention naturally drifts toward the commanders, the men at the top who make the big decisions and push the operation on. But it was the men on the ground who did the hard work of fighting on D-Day and beyond.

The British and American armies were quite different beasts, shaped by different cultures, traditions, and experiences of war. This shaped the sort of men serving in them.

Britain had a long tradition as a colonial power with a large standing army used to hold territory around the world. Britain's officer class had a certain prestige, even when commanding ordinary infantry units.

The professionalism of this military tradition had been hardened by the experience of war. The Battle of France and the retreat through Dunkirk; the failed intervention in Greece; years of fighting in North Africa; the Italian campaign –had all provided British troops with valuable battlefield experience. The pool of available manpower was more limited than in the American forces, and so men in all parts of the British military were likely to be repeatedly exposed to combat. Not every British soldier who landed on D-Day was a veteran, but the proportion of experienced men involved in Overlord was high.

The British forces included elements from the colonies and Commonwealth. For D-Day, this included a large force of Canadians. Like the British, the Canadians didn't have limitless resources, and so military prisons and hospitals had been scoured for men who could be put into action.

In the United States, which had long kept a small army and a policy of non-intervention, the military tradition was far less strong. There was pride in military service, but it wasn't as ingrained in the national culture. Specialist parts of the military were more prestigious than the infantry and had drawn of a disproportionate volume of the best men and resources, even during the early years of the war.

The bulk of the American forces were fresh-faced new soldiers, brought in as volunteers or through the military draft. A far smaller proportion of both men and officers had combat experience. Though the Americans recognized their limitations in this regard, there was little - they could do about it except to keep training the men pouring off the boats into southern England.

The main weapons of the infantry assaulting the beaches were rifles. The fundamental design of these weapons had changed little since the First World War, though they had become lighter and shorter. In modern warfare, a lot of the fighting was at short range, with men fighting in broken groups rather than massed ranks, and so weapons were optimized for this.

British soldiers carried the Lee-Enfield No.4 Mk I. The latest redesign in a series of related weapons. It was a bolt action rifle with a long sight for accuracy.

The Americans' main weapon was the M1 Garand Rifle. This was a more complex and expensive weapon than the Lee-Enfield, reflecting America's greater resources. A semi-automatic weapon, it automatically chambered a new bullet after each shot, avoiding the need to manually load as on a bolt action.

Some automatic weapons were also used, such as the M1 submachine gun and the Bren light machine gun. The lighter the weapon, the less firepower had, and so there was a balance between portability and firepower.

Armor was minimal, generally limited to a helmet to protect the head. The soldiers' fighting equipment was rounded out with bayonets for close combat and grenades for clearing out defended positions.

Aside from the infantry, the most important part of the ground forces was tanks. These became popular in the Second World War, with fast-moving armored formations sweeping across Poland and France. They were innovative, and allowed swift, decisive assaults.

The American M4 tank, known as the General Sherman, dominated. Crewed by five men and with a speed of 26 miles per hour, the Sherman went into production in 1941. It was produced in great numbers by the Americans, who supplied it to the British to serve alongside their vehicles.

Adaptations allowed tanks to make amphibious landings, coming off transport craft and straight up onto the beaches. A collapsible canvas screen was attached around the hull of a Sherman and filled with compressed air, allowing it to float. Two propellers drove it forward through the water. Once the tank landed, the canvas was deflated, creating a free firing view. This adapted vehicle was named the Duplex Drive tank.

Specialist military vehicles also played a part. For example, combat vehicles fitted with rotating flails could be used to clear mines. But it was the ordinary tank, and especially the Sherman, that would provide the heavy firepower to carry the Allies off the beaches.

In the air, the most renowned planes were still the Spitfires and Hurricanes with which the British had won the Battle of Britain. These swift, effective fighters had a fearsome reputation. But the aerial arms race was a fast-moving one, and it was a more modern plane that would prove decisive in Normandy.

The American P-51 Mustang had initially been a disappointing weapon. But when its Allison engine was replaced with a Rolls-Royce Merlin, its performance dramatically improved. It's great range, and combat ability let it effectively support the bombers attacking Germany and in doing so whittle down the German air defenses ready for D-Day. During the landings, it acted as both an interceptor, taking out enemy planes as they came for the Allied ground forces, and a ground attack craft, strafing German infantry with its six machine guns.

Amphibious landing vehicles were used to bring the infantry ashore. Experience in the Pacific had taught the Allies some valuable lessons in the use of these vehicles. It was best for men to unload from the front so they could advance up the beach quickly. But the moment the front armor dropped, those inside became vulnerable. Officers, therefore, had to take positions near the rear or risk becoming the first casualties and leaving their men without leadership.

Armed, trained, and ready, the Allied troops poured into their transport ships on the night of 5 June, ready to be carried across the Channel. But what came next didn't just depend on them. It depended upon the forces waiting on the other side of the Channel.

Chapter 6 – The German Defenses

The Germans had put huge effort into defending the territory they had conquered. Over the course of four years, from the fall of France to D-Day, they worked on a series of defenses meant to protect the entire coastline of northwest Europe, from the Pyrenees to the Arctic Circle. By June 1944, this Atlantic Wall included 12,247 fortifications, half a million beach obstacles, and 6.5 million land mines. The threats stirred up in the German imagination by Operation Bodyguard encouraged further efforts of this sort.

Anywhere the Allies landed, they would face beaches full of obstacles and explosives, guarded by armed men in concrete fortifications. This was particularly true along the Channel coast, as this was where Hitler believed an attack was most likely. He was determined to hold the Allies as they landed, prevent them from getting inland, and throw them back into the sea.

In August 1943, the defenses in Normandy were strengthened by deliberate flooding in the area around

Caen. This was a tactic that had been used in the Low Countries during both World Wars, flooded ground impeding enemy movement. The developments around Caen gave the Allies pause for thought and were initially seen as a potentially serious hindrance to Overlord, then in its early planning stages.

Though few on either side were aware of it, the defenses in the target area were weaker than they might have been. As with many other German military construction projects, slave labor had been used in building the Atlantic Wall along the Calvados coast. In some places, the laborers had acted as saboteurs, deliberately weakening the buildings they were constructing.

By late 1943, the troop formations manning these defenses were also being undermined. The war in the east was proving a huge drain on German manpower. As the year ended, 179 German divisions were serving on the Eastern Front, compared with 53 occupying the whole of France and the Low Countries. By the time the invasion came, this number had increased, but only slightly – from 53 divisions to 59.

With the Eastern Front an active warzone, it was unsurprising that men were syphoned off to fight there. Many of those who could be spared from fighting the USSR were seeing service in Italy, where the Allies continued to press against German defensive lines. Most of the toughest troops were already in action and so not available to man the Atlantic Wall. Those units stationed in France were weakened, as the best troops were taken to fight elsewhere. Resources were not allocated to them as readily as to other units.

This began to change in November 1943 with Hitler Directive 51. Such directives had the full force of law and had to be obeyed by those who received them.

Directive 51 acknowledged an Allied invasion was coming in the west. Hitler believed if the planned Allied invasion could be stopped, the possibility of a western front being created would end. He could divert troops back to the east while superweapons such as V1 rockets bombarded England into submission.

Thanks to Directive 51, renewed efforts were made to train the troops, complete the defenses, and move soldiers west. Those sent from the Eastern Front brought with them combat experience, but the men were often weary and the units undermanned. There might have been more troops in June than there had been in January, but it wasn't a huge increase.

The quality of these troops was extremely variable. Many men who had not been selected to be sent east. Some were old, young, or suffering from injuries sustained in the East. Cynicism and poor spirits prevailed. Others were far more dedicated. The SS units, a politically driven elite within the German armed forces, were dedicated to their role and determined. Hitler depended on them. The Panzer tank forces were expected to provide the vital counter-strike against the invasion.

Alongside these German troops were many others who fought for the Third Reich not out of dedication to Germany but out of belief in Nazism or position to other governments. Russians, Poles, Indians, and a range of Eastern Europeans all manned places in the Atlantic Wall.

They were less motivated to fight against the Americans and British than their comrades were. After all, theirs wasn't the nation with an empire at stake.

Overseeing the defenses was Erwin Rommel, known as the Desert Fox. A bold leader, Rommel made a name for himself during the First World War. On the Italian front, he led a detachment of men in an attack across the mountains around the Isonzo Valley, defeating and capturing forces that far outnumbered his own. Between the wars, he remained an infantry commander before becoming an instructor and the author of a best-selling book entitled *Infantry Tactics*.

Hitler was a fan of *Infantry Tactics* and made Rommel the head of his security unit. Rommel accompanied the dictator through the early days of the war and was rewarded with the command of his choice – leading a Panzer division.

At the head of his new tank division, Rommel led a decisive assault into France in May 1940, advancing at incredible speed. Leading from the front, he proved an inspiration to his men.

After France, Rommel transferred to North Africa, where he rebuilt Axis forces following a disastrous campaign by the Italians. His bold maneuvers, use of intelligence, and grasp of the potential of tanks saw the Allies driven back on several occasions. When Africa fell to the overwhelming weight of the newly arrived Americans, he took part in the defense of Italy before being moved on to plan the defense of France.

In November 1943, Rommel took over the Atlantic Wall. This led to a resurgence in work on the defenses. Four million mines were laid in four months. Anti-glider obstacles were set up along the coast. Training exercises were conducted. Rousing speeches were given. Rommel's presence was a grave issue for the Allies, partly because of his skill as a commander and because he reflected renewed German interest in bolstering northern France.

By June 1944, Rommel's presence and the activities triggered by Hitler Directive 51 had done much to bolster the German forces in Normandy. A week before D-Day, the 352nd Infantry Division, battle-hardened veterans of the Eastern Front, arrived to man the defenses around one of the landing beaches.

But there were limits on how much Rommel could achieve. Hitler's management of his subordinates through a strategy of divide and conquer was a hindrance to the smooth running of operations in France. None on the ground could claim overall control. Rommel was unable to give orders to reserves needed to stop the invasion. Hitler would not let Rommel place tank divisions close to the beaches, where the general believed they would be best placed, nor allow him to retreat and form a defensive line back from the coast. Hamstrung in his tactics, and with his belief in the potential for victory faltering, Rommel's moods became increasingly erratic.

As the invasion approached, timing took a hand. In early June, believing the Allies had missed their best opportunity, Rommel returned to Germany for his wife's birthday. While there, he was scheduled to meet with Hitler on 6 June to discuss the Atlantic Wall. At the same time, Sepp Dietrich, one of the best German tank commanders, was in Brussels, away from his 1st SS Panzer Corps. Most of the Seventh

Army's senior officers were away from their posts, attending war games in Rennes.

At that moment, the Germans were vulnerable to attack.

Chapter 7 – The Paratrooper Landings

While most of the invasion forces were being loaded into their boats on 5 June, 24,000 paratroopers were waiting to take a far faster but no less dangerous journey across the Channel.

Two forms of transport carried the paratroopers to their landing points. Some were crammed into gliders, which were towed by planes to their targets before making rough landings in Normandy. This was dangerous and difficult work, and the casualty rate among glider pilots on D-Day was high, but it allowed heavier equipment and more troops to be brought in. The journeys of the other soldiers fulfilled the classic image of the paratrooper drop. Dozens of men crammed into noisy planes, barely able to hold a shouted conversation with their neighbors. Everything they needed was strapped to them, including support weapons and bulky radio sets. As they reached their targets, they would leap out in midair and parachute to the ground below.

As the first wave of planes swept in, many pilots became nervous about German anti-aircraft fire. The small number of planes lost shows that the German batteries were largely ineffective, but there was no way for the pilots to know this at the time. They swerved through the skies, throwing around their cargos of soldiers. Confusion arose as they tried to find their targets in the dark, and men were scattered across miles of French countryside, many far from their drop zones. Those who found the right place set up lights to signal the landing zones to later aircraft, making it easier to drop troops in the right place, but the operation got off to an inauspicious start.

One of the most daring parts of this plan was Operation Titanic. Despite its grand name, Titanic only involved ten soldiers, paratroopers from Britain's elite Special Air Service (SAS). What made the operation important was how and where they landed.

Just after midnight, the first of three Titanic drop teams landed on the Cotentin peninsula, miles from the rest of the army's drop sites and landing beaches. As well as the ten commandos, hundreds of specially made dummies called Ruperts were dropped. The Ruperts were crudely made, designed only to look like a paratrooper in the dark as they fell, and contained self-destruct mechanisms that would destroy the evidence of a fake after they landed. Five hundred of them parachuted down alongside the SAS men.

On the ground, the men let off fireworks and played gramophone records of gunfire, exaggerated to increase their volume. They set up lights to indicate a drop zone being prepared.

This distraction succeeded in drawing the Germans' attention. The German 915th Infantry Regiment, the main reserves near Omaha beach, headed away from the coast to deal with the threat of a non-existent paratrooper landing. Those ten SAS soldiers had an impact out of proportion to the size of their forces, but they also suffered disproportionate losses – only two of them made it home.

The main British paratrooper force was the British 6th Airborne Division. Consisting of 8,000 men. It was dropped east of Caen. It was to capture bridges across the River Orne, preventing German Panzer forces from coming in from the east and hitting the left flank of the seaborne forces.

The first wave of British paratroopers landed too far east. But their arrival came as a surprise to the Germans, giving them the initiative. They seized the village of Ranville and moved closer to the bridges, where they secured a landing zone. Two hours after the initial drops they were joined by troops in gliders, including anti-tank guns. Now close to the bridges, they captured all but one of them and fought off a counter-attack by the German 716th Division.

The remaining bridge at Troarn was a strategically important one, as it carried the main road between Caen, Le Havre, and Rouen. Seeing the need to deal with it, Major Rosveare assembled a team, explosives, and a jeep. They raced to the bridge and blew it up, cutting the last German route across that stretch of the river.

Out at the coast, 150 British paratroopers landed near the battery at Merville, which overlooked Sword beach. They attacked the battery, resulting in fierce hand to hand fighting in which half of the unit was lost. By the end, the battery was theirs, and they had destroyed the guns.

The 16,000 American paratroopers of the 82nd and 101st Airborne Divisions had a rougher time than their British counterparts. Their job was to land at the base of the Cotentin peninsula and stop any counter-attack toward the beaches by German troops stationed at Cherbourg. Like the British, they had to secure transport routes, in this case the causeways across the flooded ground behind the landing beaches.

Clouds and anti-aircraft fire scattered the 101st Airborne over a wide area. Some paratroopers landed in swampy ground, were dragged down by the weight of their equipment, and drowned before they could even get out of their harnesses. Only one in six of the men landed close enough to reach their rendezvous point. Less than half the gliders managed to hit the drop zone, and damage sustained in their landings led to the loss of valuable equipment.

The 82nd also struggled, though not as badly. After landing, they captured St Mére-Eglise on the Cherbourg road, the first town to be liberated by the Allies.

Scattered as they were, the paratroopers were unable to secure the bridges across the River Merderet that were among their targets. But they were determined to do the best they could in difficult circumstances. Men cut off from their units joined up with other formations. They attacked German troops wherever they found them, ambushing the enemy as they raced through the darkness, trying to work out what was happening. Lieutenant-General Falley, head of the German 91ˢᵗ Division, was among those killed by the wandering paratroopers.

Falley was killed while driving back to his headquarters from the wargames at Rennes. His movements were part of a frantic mass of activity as the Germans tried to work out what was happening.

The first paratroopers had landed just after midnight, but it wasn't until 1:30 a.m. that word of a possible invasion reached the German Seventh Army headquarters. At 3:00 a.m., word was sent to the military high command in Germany that an airborne invasion was underway, though the discovery of some of the Rupert dummies was creating confusion about whether this was real and what was happening. At 4:00 a.m., General Kraiss sent a cycle regiment in the wrong direction, tricked by the dummy paratroopers.

The absence of senior commanders added to the chaos. Tank formations that were crewed and ready by 2:00 a.m. were not deployed until 8:00 a.m. Self-propelled artillery was sent out for a counter-attack, only to be withdrawn as it headed up the road. The report that this was a major invasion was sent to Berlin at 6:00a.m., but critical reserves weren't released for another ten hours.

The invasion had begun. Though the paratrooper landings were chaotic for the Allies, this was nothing compared to the chaos on the other side of the lines. Despite its problems, D-Day was off to a good start.

Chapter 8 – Omaha

The most difficult and costly of the seaborne landings took place on one of the American beaches, codenamed Omaha.

Omaha had been chosen because of its strategically important location. That stretch of the coast needed to be taken to link the other American beach, Utah, in the west, with the beaches targeted by British and Canadian forces.

Due to its terrain, Omaha was an unpleasant choice. Three hundred yards of exposed sandy beach led up to a steep shingle bank that the troops would have to ascend. Beyond that, a sea wall and sand dunes were topped off with a 150-foot plateau on which the Germans had built defensive positions. At either end of the plateau, 100-foot cliffs blocked the way. The only exits from the beach were four ravines piercing the face of the plateau, and each of these was well defended by German troops.

To make matters worse, the bombing that preceded the landings was hindered by cloud cover. Forced to attack through the clouds, the American Liberator heavy bombers feared dropping their bombs too far short of the targets and so hitting the invasion fleet. To avoid this, they had erred on the side of caution. Hundreds of tons of high explosives had been dropped just beyond Omaha beach, but instead of striking the German forward defenses they had hit the fields behind them. The German defenses remained largely intact.

American soldiers who are wading onto the Fox Green section of Omaha Beach (Normandie, France) on the morning of June 6, 1944. Artist: Chief Photographer's Mate Robert F. Sargent.

The bombardment from air and sea stopped in time for the landings. But because of delays in the troops setting out, this created a gap between the bombardment and the assault, time for the Germans to recover and start firing on the approaching craft. As the American forces approached the shore, rocket ships opened fire to support them, but many of the shots fell short, hitting landing craft.

A north-westerly wind hit the coast as the landing craft approached. At least ten vessels were swamped by waves and sank, many of their occupants drowning. A similar fate met the crews of tanks as they left their transports too far off shore. On many of them, the amphibious gear failed, the vehicles sinking and taking their crews with them. Attempts to land artillery from amphibious craft also ended in disaster.

The failures in launching the tanks meant that the infantry hit the beaches without the armored support and so withstood the worst of the initial assault. There was no subtlety to the plan they had been given, no attempt to use maneuvers to seize the routes off the beach. It would be a headlong assault into enemy fire, much like those that had characterized the First World War.

The Americans decided to deploy their landing craft 12 miles off shore, unlike the less cautious British who chose seven miles. As a result, it took three hours for most of the attackers to reach shore. Drenched in sea spray and stepping in the vomit of their sea-sick comrades, it might almost have been a relief when the front gates opened and they could get out of the craft.

Any sense of relief swiftly turned to horror as they made their way onto the beach. German firepower from the cliffs above inflicted heavy casualties. Some men weighed down by 68 pounds of equipment, drowned before they reached the shore.

Reaching land, most men sought cover. Most of the obstacles on the beach remained intact, untouched either by the preliminary bombardment or by the engineers now struggling to make it safely to shore. And so, the obstacles designed to hinder the Americans became their shelters. Paralyzed by fear, men crouched behind what cover they could find, praying for deliverance from this nightmare.

The American forces were now pinned down on the beach. Machine-gun and artillery fire meant it took extraordinary courage to try to advance. They did not have the specialist anti-tank vehicles the British used, and most of the bulldozers meant to clear obstacles had been lost in the landings, along with 40% of the engineers trained to clear the way. Seeing their troops stuck in a bloody trap, Bradley and the other commanders began to worry about whether they would ever make it off the beach. Montgomery even suggested the remaining troops might be redirected to another beach.

Yet among all this mayhem, there were some small signs of progress. An infantry company from the second wave of landings was blown off course but reached the sea wall and picked its way through the minefield beyond. Together with a group of Rangers, these men reached the plateau and stopped a counter-attack being launched against the men on the beach.

Further east, two battalions used the smoke from burning undergrowth and buildings as cover. By the time the German artillery found the range on their position, they were off the beach.

Throughout the morning, a traffic jam developed on Omaha beach, as newly arrived troops became trapped behind those already there. But those who had managed to press inland, away from the beach, started to chip away at the

Germans in their pillbox positions. Not enough men had reached the high ground to achieve a breakthrough, but they at least divided the forces and attention of the defenders.

Seeing that extreme measures were needed to break through, General Huebner, commander of the 1st Infantry Division, called for a renewed naval bombardment. The ships sailed in so close rifle fire hit some of the ships. The navy began to shell the enemy positions. With the forces so close, there was a risk of hitting their own men. But if something didn't change, the troops on the beach were dead anyway.

While the Germans had the manpower and defenses to hold up the Americans, they lacked any reserves with which to launch a counter-attack. The 915th Regiment had been drawn off by the paratrooper landings. While the 352nd and 716th Divisions together represented more troops than the Allies had counted on being there, they were still outnumbered. As the heroism of individual American soldiers led to small breakthroughs and advances, there was no way to push them back. Bit by bit, the Americans began working their way up the ravines, until at last a breakout was achieved.

By 11:00 a.m., enough American troops had pressed forward inland to capture nearby Vierville. While some men kept up the fight against the defenses at the top of the plateau, others began to make their way cautiously off the beach. Bulldozers and explosives were turned to the task of clearing the obstacles and minefields blocking their way.

One by one, the German positions above Omaha beach were destroyed, either by the shelling of naval guns or by determined and courageous attacks by small bands of soldiers. At 1:30 p.m. Major-General Gerow signaled to Bradley the men previously trapped on the beach were making their way inland.

As the Germans responded to the growing crisis up and down the coast, they made a crucial error of judgment. The American forces at Omaha had achieved only a shallow beachhead and taken heavy losses along the way. If the Allies could be driven back into the sea, it was here. But instead of focusing on Omaha, the German commanders hurried to bring their reserves to bear against the British and Canadians who had landed further east. One battalion of infantry was sent to tackle the American paratroopers in the Cotentin peninsula. Another lone battalion was sent to stem the tide of Americans pouring out of Omaha beach. It was not nearly enough.

By dusk, the beachhead stretched only 1,200 yards inland. The Americans had not reached their D-Day objectives, though they were now within a mile of them. They settled down to hold the ground they had taken.

The great cost and struggle that had gone into taking Omaha beach led to a change of plans in what was unloaded that night. Instead of quickly building up supplies on the beach to support the troops who had already landed, the bare minimum was landed to see them through the night. The focus was on bringing more troops ashore to keep up the fight. Exhausted sailors worked long into the night, bringing more of the fighting force off the transport ships and onto dry land.

At Omaha, the Allies had come closer to defeat than anywhere else in the D-Day landings. But perseverance and courage saw them through.

Chapter 9 – Utah

There was a huge contrast in the experience of the troops on the two American beaches, for both the attackers and the defenders. Utah was more orderly and far less costly for the Americans. But its end results, much like those on Omaha, were a disappointment for the ambitious Allied commanders.

German forces at Utah beach were far less substantial than at Omaha. As with so much about the defense of Normandy, this stemmed from a lack of understanding on the German side of what the Allies would want from the geography of their landing zones and how they would use the terrain to their advantage.

Behind Utah beach, flooded and marshy ground would constrict the movement of troops in from the coast. Only a limited number of causeways would allow tanks to move inland and men to make their way in without wading through deep waters. It was ground that could have been designed to slow down an invasion.

But Utah had critical advantages. It was a large enough beach to accommodate the landing of tens of thousands of men and their supplies, as well as tank and support vehicles. The flatness that contributed to the flooded lands beyond meant a relatively easy ascent up the beach. And strategically, its position near the neck of the Cotentin Peninsula would allow the Allies to gain control of the peninsula and the port of Cherbourg.

The relatively small force of Germans holding Utah beach was in for a terrible shock on the morning of 6 June. Three hundred and sixty Marauder medium bombers stormed out of the heavens, raining their payload down on the German emplacements. The Marauder was one of the best American bombers of the war, hard to take down and with heavy armaments for a plane of its size. The Marauders were followed by a remarkably accurate naval bombardment. Eighteen Allied warships lying off the coast opened fire, destroying many of the heavy guns and concrete bunkers the Germans were relying on. German troops pulled back into defensive positions, manned what heavy weapons remained, and waited for the inevitable assault.

The initial American assault came in four waves. The first was meant to be a formation of 32 amphibious tanks from the 70th Tank Battalion, followed by three waves of infantry. As at Omaha, the infantry was placed in their landing craft 12 miles off coast and suffered through a three-hour journey in vehicles best suited to short trips from ship to shore. As at Omaha, it was a salt-encrusted and often sea-sick force that reached the beach.

Better luck and weaker German resistance meant more troops did make it safely to the beach. Of 32 tanks, 28 made the journey from their transport craft intact, a far better result than in the disastrous tank landings at Omaha. But a strong headwind delayed their arrival by 20 minutes. Instead of arriving before the infantry, and so providing them with cover and support from the start, they landed after the first wave of troops had already hit the beach.

That first wave arrived at 6.30 a.m. Currents off shore brought the landing craft in further south than had been intended, leading to even weaker resistance. This was the most lightly defended part of the whole Normandy coast and the Germans had been suitably softened up. As the men waded 500 yards to the shore, only minimal fire hit them. Most made it safely onto the beach.

Then came the tanks. The shocked Germans saw machines rising out of the water, like so many sea monsters emerging from the ocean depths. Tank guns joined infantry fire, knocking out concrete defensive emplacements and the guns they held.

Desultory artillery and machine-gun fire hit the Americans as they advanced. The infantry made swift progress, taking on the few defenders and clearing the way for the further waves of troops as they arrived. Many of the Germans, seeing they were badly outnumbered, chose to surrender rather than fight on against overwhelming odds.

While the first waves of infantry advanced up the beach, engineers set to work clearing the way for the men and vehicles that would follow. They defused mines and blew up obstacles, creating a path the tanks could get through.

At Omaha, each thing that went wrong had led to more problems. The loss of engineers and bulldozers on the way to the beach meant they struggled to clear away the defenses. The defenses and loss of tanks hindered the advance off the beach to take out the Germans, meaning that the engineers and the rest of the men trapped with them took even heavier casualties.

At Utah, success bred further success. The ease of the landings and the advance up the beach made it easier for the engineers to do their job, making further advances simpler and safer. Within three hours of the first landings, paths had been cleared for tanks to drive up the beach, secure the causeways beyond, and support an advance inland.

Meanwhile, the American infantry had found five routes off the beach, one undefended ahead of them and four more at the western end, where the Germans put up little fight. They began heading inland.

While Utah had provided the easiest landing, it also provided the most difficult terrain for an advance away from the coast. The causeways funneled men and tanks down a couple of narrow routes. The Germans heavily defended the end of one of the causeways, destroying a bridge that was part of the route. Engineers had to carry out repairs and remove damaged vehicles before the tanks could complete their journey.

Many men were forced to sit and wait for hours, staying in what cover they could find in case of enemy fire. Rather than wait to join the narrow causeway advances, some infantry headed off through the flooded land. It was a slow and unpleasant journey as they waded along, weapons raised above their heads. The water ruined prized cartons of cigarettes. Engineers marked out paths for the infantry with white tape, but even so, some men stumbled into hidden ditches and almost drowned.

German resistance stiffened as the Americans headed further inland. But the paratroopers who had landed in the area, and with whom the Utah forces were meant to link up, created confusion and distraction among the Germans.

By the end of the day, forces from Utah had advanced six miles inland. They hadn't completed their task of linking up with the 82nd and 101st Airborne, nor had they reached all their objectives. But they had landed 23,000 troops on a defended coast, taking only 197 casualties in the process. More men were lost in vessels sunk by the Germans than in the fighting for the beach itself.

The Americans had one chaotic landing and one highly successful one. Further east, the British and Canadians were experiencing less extreme conditions as they made their landings.

Chapter 10 – Gold

Gold Beach was the westernmost of the British invasion beaches, the point at which the Anglo-Canadian forces would meet the Americans of the Omaha beachhead. A stretch of coastline between Port-en-Bessin in the west and La Rivière in the east, steep cliffs overlooked its western end. As a result, the actual landing zone ran from Le Hamel to La Rivière.

Gold Beach was reasonably well defended by the Germans. There were seven defensive strongholds, each designed to be held by 50 men, as well as two substantial but partially constructed artillery emplacements that provided shelter for heavy guns. As on the other beaches, a range of obstacles stood in the way of the men emerging from the sea. Land mines, anti-tank obstacles, wooden stakes, and metal tripods were combined with barbed wire to create a difficult and dangerous approach. Believing the Allies would arrive at high tide, reducing the amount of time troops spent advancing up the beach, Rommel ordered these obstructions be focused around the high tide line.

At 5.30 a.m., the naval bombardment began. Allied ships sitting off the coast battered away at the gun emplacements above Gold Beach, with light and medium bombers also contributing to the attack. Self-propelled guns aboard the landing craft added to the barrage, though these were not as effective as had been hoped.

Several of the German heavy guns were taken out, but some remained. The bombers failed to crack a gun emplacement at Le Hamel, leaving it free to fire on the western end of the Allied landings.

The remaining guns and gusts of wind made for a rough ride onto Gold Beach. Sea mines made things worse. Of five landing craft carrying the 47 Commandos to the beach, three were destroyed by mines, leaving the surviving commandos to swim for shore.

The landings began at 7.25 a.m., nearly an hour after the Americans began their landings up the coast. The tides had dictated when was best for each landing, preventing them from all coming at once.

Tanks were supposed to accompany the first landings, but this proved difficult. Rough seas meant the tanks had to deploy closer to land than had been planned and their arrival on the beach was delayed. The first wave of infantry thus had to manage without them, many taking cover behind pieces of the German beach defenses.

The tanks used on Gold Beach were more varied than those on the American beaches. While the Americans liked to use large numbers of identical vehicles, the British liked to experiment with specialist vehicles. As well as the armored bulldozers needed for clearing defenses, there were tanks with flamethrowers to burn out troops from well-defended positions and others with giant rotating flails which could be used to explode mines ahead of the tank, clearing a path for others to follow.

Self-propelled guns approached the beach, firing from their landing craft as they went. When they got near, gunners dressed only in underwear and gym shoes leapt into the sea to deploy mats referred to as "roly-polies", which the vehicles could drive up to get onto the shore. With German guns blazing and the wind threatening to drag their landing craft onto mines, the gunners struggled to maneuver the unwieldy roly-polies into place. Despite these efforts, many tanks became bogged down or were destroyed by German fire before they could advance up the beach, especially at the western end.

Engineers and mine-clearing tanks began clearing routes up the beach. Meanwhile, men ran from the exposed open sand into the greater cover provided by the dunes. As they progressed up the beach, they fought Germans defending trenches and pillboxes. Within a few hours, they were making advances inland.

Gold Beach saw one of the most extraordinary displays of courage on D-Day, and indeed throughout the war.

Sergeant Major Stanley Hollis was a member of the Green Howards, an infantry regiment from northern England. Veterans of the fighting in the Middle East, North Africa, and Italy, the Howards had impressed Montgomery with their courage and tenacity and so were chosen to be part of the first wave of troops to land.

As a member of D Company of the 6th Green Howards, Hollis led a detachment under heavy fire up Gold Beach. After fighting enemy troops hidden behind a hedge, they crossed a minefield and spotted a German pillbox on the far side. This was the source of the heavy fire that they and others in the area had been suffering.

Sten gun blazing, Hollis single-handedly charged the pillbox, drawing the enemy's fire away from his comrades in arms, and defeated the Germans inside. After taking a second pillbox, Hollis learned about a vital gun emplacement, which he led his men against.

As the Howards advanced inland, Hollis ran up against a group of well emplaced German soldiers. When an attack against them failed, he went back to retrieve two men who had been left behind in the retreat.

Even amid the other acts of courage on D-Day, Hollis's persistent presence in the heart of the action drew attention and he was awarded the Victoria Cross, the highest honor available to British service personnel.

On D-Day afternoon, Hollis and the Howards weren't the only ones heading inland from Gold Beach. British forces advancing from the beach took control of the road to Bayeux, seizing the village of Ryes. Though they didn't get as far as Bayeux itself, and like all the Allied forces they didn't reach all their D-Day goals, they made significant advances. Forces were diverted to taking out the Germans at Le Hamel, reducing advances in other areas.

Meanwhile, 47th Royal Marine Commando had a specific task for the day. This force of 420 men was to arrive on the beach at 9.25 a.m. and head out west. Their target was the small harbor of Port-en-Bessin, at the boundary with the American Omaha sector. Because the harbor was well defended from the seaward side, they would attack it from the south, securing it as a landing place for the Allies.

The Port-en-Bessin expedition got into trouble before it even hit the beach. Several of 47 Commando's landing craft were hit by mines, causing 76 casualties. Some men became separated from the rest. Those who remained gathered and headed for their target, but were slowed down by heavy skirmishes with Axis troops. By the time they reached the launch point for their attack, a ridge south of Port-en-Bessin, it was ten thirty at night and too late to continue. They dug in for the night. The next day, they would launch their attack, taking the town in two days of fighting.

The landings on Gold Beach had been largely successful. Though certain key targets for the day, such as Port-en-Bessin and Bayeux, remained in enemy hands, the beach had been taken, and significant progress had been made inland. 25,000 men had come ashore, of whom around a thousand had been killed or injured. They were ready to link up with the Americans in the west and so join up the Allied front.

But the most significant target, and the place of greatest German resistance lay beyond the other British beach. And between that and Gold lay the Canadians.

Chapter 11 – Juno

Responsibility for taking Juno beach fell upon the Canadian army. The size and prestige of the American and British military forces means that the Canadians have often been neglected in accounts of the Second World War. But just as in the First World War, they faced challenges as great as those of the other Allies, displaying every bit as much courage, skill, and tenacity as their comrades in arms. As at the other beaches, the naval forces supporting the operation were also a reminder of the remarkable international nature of the coalition facing Germany, with the Allied fleet including Canadian, British, Free French, and Free Norwegian vessels.

Juno was one of the more strongly defended beaches. The usual mass of obstacles blocked the way up the beach at the high-water mark. Behind them, there were strongpoints every thousand yards, involving machine-gun posts, artillery positions, and bunkers. These were defended by the 716th Static Infantry Division, a unit which was mostly made up of very young or old soldiers, but which was still considered better than average for a division of its type.

Panzer forces and eastern European conscripts were stationed inland.

The Juno landing ran into difficulties before the men even hit the beach.

The usual bombardment by air and sea preceded the arrival of troops. This bombardment included the use of obsolete Centaur tanks carrying 95mm howitzers and providing covering fire from their landing craft. But the combination of landing vessels and the firing tanks turned out to be far less seaworthy than had been hoped. Scores of them sank, and only six made it to shore to support the infantry.

Meanwhile, a reef off the beach provided an obstacle to all the landing craft. The advance was delayed, and the pilots struggled to coordinate as they crossed the difficult waters.

When the infantry hit the beach, they landed amid the obstacles laid out by the Germans. They also arrived without the tank support they had been expecting, as the difficulties at sea meant many of the amphibious tanks and the specialist obstacle clearing tanks were held back.

Having deposited the troops, the craft were meant to pull out. But they became caught up in the German defenses, steel obstructions and mines preventing them from getting out. As more landing craft came in, mines damaged some, forcing the soldiers inside to get out and wade ashore. Of the first 24 landing craft, 20 were lost or damaged. For the whole morning, it was 90 out of 306.

Faced with rows of obstacles and barbed wire, under fire from the German troops in their defensive positions, the

Canadians began advancing up the beach. Their experience varied hugely from one part of Juno to another. Some units came under heavy fire and quickly became worn down. Others had an easier time and could start tackling the obstacles in their way.

Meanwhile, the first tanks onto the beach opened fire on the German strongpoints, hoping to destroy tough concrete emplacements that had survived the preparatory bombardment.

In some parts of the beach, the Canadians became pinned down by German fire. At the east end, even the 100-yard run from the boats to the cover of the sea wall proved costly due to heavy enemy fire. The shortage of tanks meant that the infantry lacked the heavy support that they needed to advance. They couldn't clear out the Germans and so make the beach safe for obstacles and mines to be cleared and a path created for the vehicles. Troops became backed up on the sands.

Breakthroughs came in different ways in different places. Commandos risked heavy casualties to rush up the beach and into action. One of the supporting ships came in close to shore and hammered the defenders at the east end of the beach with its guns, providing a way off the beach. Demolition bombs, tanks, and other heavy weapons took out strongpoints, though often at a high cost.

By the early afternoon, the breakthroughs had been made and the Canadians were engaged with the second line of German defenses, inland from the beach itself. As they advanced, they ran into fresh difficulties.

Some units were held back by the loss of equipment on the way to the beach. Supplies had been lost with damaged or destroyed landing craft. Some bulky equipment had been abandoned as men struggled to make it onto the beach.

German snipers played a part. Placed in carefully chosen positions, they began picking off soldiers as they advanced. All the troops that landed on D-Day had to face a choice – whether to tackle isolated snipers, and so slow down their advance, or to keep moving, letting the snipers remain behind them and accepting the casualties this would likely cause. The Canadians kept moving on past, not letting these isolated assassins pin them down.

It was one thing to advance across a beach and through open fields. It was quite another to face the enemy in the coastal villages that dotted the landscape. These provided defensive positions for the German troops, with plenty of cover and hiding places. At Courselles, street fighting bogged down the advance through most of the afternoon. At St Aubin, it took three hours to drive out the last Germans. At Bernières, half an assault company was lost in the hundred-yard advance from landing points to the village, and the enemy clung tenaciously to their position until they were eventually outflanked.

At Tailleville, tanks advanced through the village, smashing German positions. But they hadn't counted on the complicated network of emplacements the defenders had built underneath the village. The Germans used these bunkers to repeatedly outflank the Canadian infantry. It was only after seven hours of fighting the village was cleared.

Having fought their way off the beaches, the Canadians went on to make the deepest advances of D-Day. Follow-up units moved past the tired troops of the first landing waves and used the routes they had established off the coast. Pushing on to their objectives, they got seven miles inland, further than any other Allied troops. They reached the road between Bayeaux and Caen, a critical artery for traffic in the region, and got within three miles of Caen, where they linked up with the British 50th Division.

Meanwhile, the assault troops around the beaches mopped up the remaining German resistance. Snipers continued to harass the Canadians until nightfall, by which time they were left isolated far behind Allied lines.

As night fell, Canadian forces dug in along a line inland from Juno beach. Their landings had been among the most successful of D-Day, despite the ineffectiveness of the preparatory bombardment and the heavy losses taken in some parts of the beach. They had sustained around 2,000 casualties. In return, they had smashed the German formations facing them, broken through the Atlantic Wall and its defensive formations, and linked up with the British at one end of their line.

Things were only going to get tougher for the Canadians. Their achievements, and those of the British to their east were drawing the attention of the Germans. There would be no easy advance on Caen.

Chapter 12 – Sword

Sword Beach, the easternmost of the landing zones, was one of the British targets. Lying closest to the city of Caen, it was a vital anchoring point for Montgomery's strategy for the following weeks. It was also the sector of the line that would most obviously demonstrate the over-ambitious nature of Allied goals for D-Day.

Sword had the same sort of defenses as the other beaches the Allies landed on. Landmines, stakes, and concrete blocks designed to stop tank advances all littered the flat, open beach, interspersed with occasional pillbox defensive emplacements. Behind that were 20 strongpoints, some containing artillery. Machine-guns and snipers were installed in former tourist homes lining the shore.

What made this part of the line different was the German reserve force based near Caen, nine miles from Sword. The 21st Panzer Division, a 16,000-strong force of tanks, mobile troops, and anti-tank troops, held positions either side of the River Orne. If they could be mobilized and brought to the fight, they could make a huge impact on the British advance.

The aerial and naval bombardment of the defenses at Sword Beach began at 3:00 a.m. The effort was concentrated around Hermanville-sur-Mer, where the landing craft could most easily reach the beach.

As the Allied bombardment pounded the German positions, troops started heading to the beach. In the forefront were the tanks, including the specialist vehicles the British referred to as "funnies," such as the mine destroyers and flame throwers.

A mile from the beach, German shells started hitting the landing craft. The craft pressed on, some in dramatic style. A bugler sounded the General Salute as he passed the command ship.

The British had an incredibly detailed plan for the waves of troops to hit the beach. First would come the amphibious tanks at 7.25 a.m. Five minutes later, landing craft would deposit specialist engineering tanks into the shallows, where they would emerge onto the beach. The first wave of infantry would arrive seven minutes later, the next thirteen minutes after that, and so on through the early hours of the landing.

The operation got off to a good start. The first waves arrived on time. As mortar and machine-gun fire rained down around them, sappers set to work demolishing obstructions. Flail tanks whipped the sand, safely setting off mines before anyone was close enough to be caught in the blast. The specialist tanks also showed they could be useful in a more general role, using their guns to take out German gun emplacements.

Some of the first men off the boats were hit immediately. But these formations who took point didn't suffer as heavy casualties as others who followed behind, pushing past them to launch advances in the face of heavy enemy fire.

The mine-clearing tanks began using their flails when they hit the high-water mark and kept going until they were off the beach. This cleared paths for others to follow. Amphibious tanks cleared the beach of any tough positions and then drove up into the dunes, where they became involved in heavy fighting.

Despite the successful start, a schedule as complex as the British landing one inevitably began to fall behind. There was no way every wave could land on time in the face of opposition. The beach became clogged with men, vehicles, and wreckage. Throughout the day, German mortars and artillery from further inland bombarded the men waiting to get off the sands and into action.

Meanwhile, a single courageous French girl waded into the blood-stained waters and helped wounded soldiers out of the shallows.

Despite German resistance, the British secured Sword Beach in less than an hour and headed inland with remarkable speed. By nine in the morning, the men of the 1st Battalion South Lancashire Regiment were over a mile inland at Hermanville.

Montgomery's aim for this force was focused on Caen. They were to advance to the city, engage with the Panzer forces there, and hold them over the following days while the Americans secured the Cotentin Peninsula. This meant a speedy advance to ensure the Panzers were fully occupied.

Commando units and men of the East Yorkshire Regiment set out from the beach to take Ouistreham and Lion-sur-Mer. Tanks rushed from the coast to pre-planned rendezvous points, past shocked Germans cowering in shell holes. Though they had fought their way through the first line, they still faced opposition. Snipers fired at exposed men. German guns of the 1716th Artillery Regiment rushed up to launch a counter-attack at Lion-sur-Mer.

The counter-attack at Lion was briefly successful. The British had not yet brought up heavy weapons and so were vulnerable to the German artillery. The Germans captured a group of British prisoners and were amazed at the quality of their supplies compared with those in blockaded Germany. But the success was short lived. The Allies brought up more troops, and the Germans were pushed back.

Their level of success surprised the British troops. They had been trained to fight on the beaches. Now they were inland, facing different conditions from those they had most prepared for. The success was gratifying but at times bewildering.

At 11:00 a.m., troops began gathering for the advance to take Caen. The initial force was meant to consist of the 2nd King's Own Shropshire Light Infantry (KSLI) and a group of tanks from the Staffordshire Yeomanry. The KSLI gathered in an orchard outside Lion, threw away their no longer needed maps of the area around the beach, and marched to Hermanville to meet the tanks.

But the tanks were stuck. An unexpectedly high tide, combined with many support vehicles on the beach, had obstructed their advance. An hour after the group was meant to set out, the KSLI started marching for Caen alone, with the tanks set to catch up later.

Meanwhile, other troops were fighting to take out two German strongpoints labelled "Morris" and "Hillman." Hillman proved particularly tough, and the 1st Battalion of the Suffolk Regiment took heavy casualties there. Looking for a way to take the position, an engineer discovered tanks could safely cross the minefields. The vehicles used explosive charges to breach the defenses, leading to the strongpoint's capture.

The KSLI fought a series of small but fierce engagements as they advanced toward Caen. Late in the afternoon, now accompanied by some of the promised tanks, they reached Biéville and again overwhelmed the Germans, this time through a flanking maneuver.

It was here, at Lebisey wood, that the British advance on Caen stalled. The first formations of the German 21st Panzer Division joined the fight. The leading company of the KSLI took heavy casualties, including the loss of their commander. Under heavy fire, they halted around 6:00 p.m. and dug in for the night. The leading company pulled back, disengaging from the Germans to take shelter with the rest of their regiment.

On a hill above Lebisey, the German General Marcks saw that, while he had halted the advance on Caen, the situation was dire. The Allies had landed in force and were pouring more troops into their bridgehead. Presciently, he said if the British could not be thrown back into the sea, Germany would lose the war.

He launched a counter-attack.

Led by Marcks himself, a German Panzer formation rushed north across open land, heading for the gap between the British and Canadian landing zones. If he could exploit that weak point, maybe he could drive the invaders back.

It was a desperate and ineffective gamble. As the Germans reached the Sherman tanks of the Staffordshires on a hill near the Caen road, they immediately lost 13 of their own tanks. By the time they reached Lion-sur-Mer, only a fragment of Marcks' original force remained. Seeing Allied gliders coming into the east, they feared they would be encircled. They withdrew toward Caen.

The result was one of mixed fortunes. The British hoped to take Caen on the first day. It was a strategically important objective, and now it was defended by the remains of Marcks' force. On the other hand, the German force lost 70 out of 124 tanks in their futile counterattack, severely weakening the defensive formation.

With minimal tank and artillery support, taking Caen on the first day was never a realistic objective for the KSLI. Given the Panzer forces in the vicinity, it might never have been plausible for the British at all. At Sword, as at the other landing zones, D-Day ended with key aims unfulfilled.

The Allies had achieved an extraordinary thing, securing a beachhead in Normandy in the face of Rommel's carefully prepared defenses. But the Germans had fought well.

As night fell and the two sides dug in, the question became, where do we go from here?

Chapter 13 – The Resistance

While the foreign soldiers landed on their north coast to liberate them, the people of France were not sitting idle. While most had no idea what was happening on the Norman coast, a significant minority knew the invasion was coming. They leapt into action to support it.

For the 100,000 men and women of the French Resistance, the call to action had come.

The Resistance first emerged in the immediate aftermath of the fall of France in 1940. Though most French people turned to the government in ostensibly free Vichy to keep their nation alive, others chose different paths. For some, this meant exile and joining General Charles de Gaulle's Free French forces in England. For others, it meant resisting the Germans from within, forming cells of freedom fighters who sought to cast out the Nazi-led invaders.

Initially, much Resistance activity consisted of attacks on German soldiers, the most direct and obvious way of hurting the occupiers. But this brought acts of sometimes terrible retribution down upon the heads of the French. And so, in time, the Resistance turned to less direct tactics.

Attacks focused on the infrastructure supporting the German troops. Supply and communication lines were attacked. Equipment was sabotaged. The men and women carrying out these attacks were still risking their lives, but the penalties for their communities, if they were caught, would be less severe.

The growth and increasing coordination of the French Resistance was supported by the work of the Allies. Britain's Special Operations Executive (SOE), America's Office of Strategic Services (OSS), and De Gaulle's Free French forces sought to work with resistance cells. They linked up with existing groups, recruited new ones, and provided supplies. They gave them radios to stay in contact with each other and the outside world.

The Resistance was never just a means of attacking the Germans. They were also a valuable source of intelligence, helping the Allies to keep on top of events in occupied France, and a part of the escape networks that helped downed pilots and men who escaped from POW camps to get out of Axis territory.

One of the most important channels of communication was Radio London. This station broadcast from Britain for an audience on the occupied continent. It sought to provide a propaganda tool against the Axis and to keep the hopes of freedom-loving Europeans alive. It also provided a way to send messages to resistance members without them needing powerful and cumbersome two-way radio sets. Resistance groups provided phrases for the authorities in Britain. When these phrases were included in the "personal messages" section of a Radio London broadcast, that told resistance cells the time had come for specific events, such as supply drops.

By the time of D-Day, the Resistance had grown massively from its original roots. Hitler's war against the USSR had put pressure on German industry, and a labor draft had been introduced in France to provide manpower. This led to greater resistance than before, as the French sought freedom from such measures. As Overlord prepared to launch, over 100,000 people were part of the resistance network.

The Americans and British did not entirely trust the Resistance or even the discretion of their Free French allies. De Gaulle was only told about D-Day two days in advance. At the start of June, the Resistance were informed, by a signal from Radio London, that the invasion was imminent.

In the months leading up the operation, the Resistance had gone into overdrive, attacking German infrastructure, in particular railway engines. On the night before D-Day, a fresh signal from Radio London told them now was the time to go all out.

The signal informed the Resistance an invasion was coming, but not the location. They sprang into action, attacking transport and communications networks that could aid the occupiers. Five hundred and seventy-seven railroads, 30 roads, and 32 telecommunications sites were destroyed. The ability of the Germans to counter the landings was severely hampered by the infrastructure damage and acts of armed insurrection across France.

Just before D-Day, the Allies began a new form of coordination with the Resistance. Jedburgh teams were three-man groups of uniformed Allied soldiers, one of them always French. They were parachuted into France with radio equipment, with the mission of joining up with Resistance groups. They helped to encourage and coordinate the Resistance, who was now officially brought under the wing of the Allied military.

The Resistance helped to make D-Day a success. But many members lost their lives as they responded to the signal only to find the Allies were weeks or even months away from reaching them with support. In the days that followed, they were active close to the battle lines, joining with regular Allied forces in a fight to free their country.

The beaches had fallen. The Allies were moving inland. The Resistance was rising ahead of them. But the battle for Normandy had only just begun.

Chapter 14 –Advance

As dawn rose on 7 June 1944, Allied forces sat in four distinct pockets on the Norman coast. The Canadians linked up with one of the British beaches, but other than that, each landing force was on its own. The longer they stayed separated from each other, the more time each group spent without the full support of the others. They were the more vulnerable for it.

One of the biggest challenges the Allied troops faced over the following weeks was the Bocage, the distinctive scenery of that part of France. Frequent hedgerows, sunken and winding roads, and tall earth banks all contributed to making a landscape that favored the defender. German guns, tanks, and infantry dug in using camouflage to hide and catch the Allies by surprise. In a single engagement, German tank ace Michael Wittman and his unit took out 27 British tanks in fighting at Villers Bocage, most of them destroyed in the initial ambush in which Wittman drove out of cover and down the length of a British formation, destroying the tanks as he passed.

While circumstances on the ground favored the Germans, those in the air were on the Allies' side. They had superiority in the air, allowing them to bomb German formations as they tried to reach the front. Close to the coast, this bombing was reinforced by bombardment from Allied ships, which could fire up to 16 miles inland. As the Allies moved away from the coast, they lost this cover but gained better close aerial support, as they established airbases close to the front lines.

The result was a steady Allied advance. The Germans could not muster a substantial counterattack, as Allied aircraft attacked any large formations they saw on the roads. But the Allies could not make swift breakthroughs, as they were bogged down fighting hedge-to-hedge and house-to-house to advance.

On the day after D-Day, a German SS Panzer force tried to launch a counter-attack. They were destroyed before they even reached the front.

While this attack was being thwarted, the British and Canadians finished linking up into a single front. The following day, Royal Marines captured Port-en-Bessin, and the day after that, the British linked up with the battered American forces at Omaha Beach. American paratroopers continued to gather together, becoming an increasingly coherent and effective force. But the Americans were struggling to bridge the gap between Omaha and Utah. It wasn't until 12 June, with an American victory in fierce fighting at Carentan, that the beachheads were all connected. The Allies now held a single swathe of territory 15 miles deep and 60 miles long.

Allied air attacks prevented the Germans from mustering a substantial force in the region. Bombers attacked trains travelling west, stopping troops long before they reached the front. SS Panzer Divisions hastily summoned from the Eastern Front were smashed before they even reached the combat lines.

The Allies had no such problems. Tens of thousands of men were ashore, and still more were coming. The number who came through the Mulberry harbors would be counted in the millions.

Supply lines to Britain were almost ruined on the 19th when the fiercest storm in 50 years tore its way up the Channel. The Mulberry harbors were smashed, one of them beyond repair, though the one at Arromanches was made functional using parts from the ruined harbor. A dozen ships were sunk, and hundreds were blown onto the shore. The Allies were left short of food and ammunition, their air cover grounded by the bad weather.

But by then Germans were well established in defensive positions. During their brief window of opportunity, no counter-attack emerged.

Having finished linking up, the Americans focused on taking the Cotentin Peninsula. The main strategic target there was the town of Cherbourg, which would give the Allies a deep-water harbor.

On 17 June, the Americans completed their advance across the neck of the peninsula. Three days later, they were within striking distance of Cherbourg. The German units there were tired and demoralized, but the commander of the garrison, Lieutenant General Karl-Wilhelm von Schlieben, refused to surrender. Instead, he sent his troops to destroy the harbor facilities so they would not fall into Allied hands.

On the 22nd, the Americans launched their attack on the city. Progress was slow at first, as the Germans were well dug in, defending concrete pillboxes and bunkers. The tipping point came on the 26th. That day, British commandos stormed the German naval intelligence headquarters, while American forces took Fort du Roule, which dominated the city. Von Schlieben was captured, and any organized defensive effort ended. The last Germans in the town were defeated on the 1st of July.

As planned, the Americans had taken the Cotentin Peninsula and were moving beyond there to advance west and south. But the British and Canadians remained stalled outside Caen. There, the Germans clung tenaciously to defensive positions around the city.

On 26 June, Montgomery launched a massive attack on Caen. Using devastating artillery power, the Allies took the critical high ground at Hill 112, south of the city. The following day, the Germans massed as many tanks as they could spare, some from the battered forces brought from the Eastern Front, others brought up from the south of France. They counterattacked at Hill 112, triggering a merciless five-day battle that saw a nearby river clogged with dead bodies.

Behind the German lines, political divisions made it hard to coordinate the military effort. Hitler's strategy for managing his subordinates meant there was no one in clear command of the forces in the region. His personal interventions were often misguided and made it difficult for commanders to effectively fight the war. Some of them, realizing the war effort was doomed, wanted to seek a negotiated peace with the Allies. Hitler refused to even consider the option, and so they began plotting an unsuccessful attempt to assassinate and replace him.

July brought heavy rain and with it bad memories. American, British, and French forces were once again bogged down in a slow, grinding war against the Germans amid the mud of northern France. Inevitably, it reminded people of the First World War, and some worried this would turn into another stalemate. In Britain, the sense of excitement that had greeted D-Day began to fade.

The Allies needed to break out of the patch of northern France in which the Germans had them contained. They began hatching a plan.

For the breakout to work, the Allies needed to ensure the British and Canadians under Montgomery were fulfilling their original purpose of occupying the German armored forces. This objective combined with the still incomplete objective of capturing Caen, resulting in a renewed attack on the city.

Two thousand, five hundred tons of bombs were dropped on Caen by the RAF, softening up the defenders ready for a big attack. The Canadians took heavy casualties assaulting the airfield at Carpiquet. The British invaded the northwest districts of the city and took them in two days of street-to-street fighting. They attacked Hill 112 again, suffering heavy casualties to take the high ground.

On 17 July, a British Spitfire strafed the car of General Rommel as he returned to his headquarters. Rommel was severely injured. He was taken to the hospital and later committed suicide after being implicated in the plot to kill Hitler. The commander of the Atlantic Wall and one of the most dynamic leaders in the German military was gone.

The next day, Montgomery launched Operation Goodwood and Operation Atlantic. These two offensives saw the British and Canadians push hard against the Germans in and around Caen. Bitter fighting followed, and by the end, the devastated city was in Allied hands.

Montgomery's approach at Caen has been criticized by many historians, who argue his tactics led to unnecessarily high losses. The battle was certainly costly for the British and Canadians. But in a broader strategic sense, it achieved its objective. All the available German armor was being poured into holding the city. To the west, where General Bradley was commanding the American ground forces, there was not the same tough armored opposition.

By late July, the Allies held a substantial bridgehead in northern France. Now it was time to go beyond that sector.

It was time for a breakout.

Chapter 15 – Breakout

Throughout the campaign so far, one figure had been notable for his absence.

General George S. Patton was one of the most controversial commanders in the U.S. Army. Bold, determined, and skilled, he had risen to prominence as a tank commander. He had led American forces to successes in North Africa, where he became a hero to many and a terror to the Germans.

Patton's strong personality could make him a liability as well as an asset. He repeatedly clashed with other commanders, especially Montgomery. During the invasion of Italy, his physical and verbal abuse of a shell-shocked soldier created a storm of outrage that saw him deprived of his command.

But Patton was too popular and skillful a commander to be kept on the bench forever. During the build up to D-Day, the Allies used his presence to add weight to the illusory First U.S. Army Group without giving him the responsibility of command. Now the fighting was on, and they needed decisive action, he was exactly the sort of man they wanted at the front.

On 6 July, Patton arrived in Normandy. Bradley, previously his subordinate, was now his superior and had summoned him to lead a swift, hard strike that would break through the German lines, drive south, and then head east, catching the enemy by surprise. Hidden away in a camouflaged bivouac in the Cotentin Peninsula, Patton began work on assembling the U.S. Third Army, which he would command for this expedition.

On 25 July, the Americans began Operation Cobra. Three thousand bombers dropped 4,000 tons of napalm, high-explosives, and fragmentation bombs on a five-mile stretch of the German lines near St-Lô. Around 70% of the German troops ended up out of action because of the bombing – dead, wounded, or too traumatized to fight.

Into the ruins of the German lines, the VII and VIII Corps of the U.S. First Army began their advance. Isolated groups of German soldiers held out stiffly against them in a landscape of charred ruins and craters. As they were forced to withdraw, the Germans left minefields and booby traps behind, inflicting further casualties.

After the first day, the pace of the advance started to improve. There were fewer Germans left to resist. Hitler had ordered them not to retreat, preventing them from making a tactical withdrawal that might have held up the American advance.

The Americans took Coutances on 27 July and Avranches on the 30th.They were making progress, but this was still not the main event.

On 30 July, Bradley unleashed Patton. The Third Army poured through the gap created for them by the VII and VIII Corps.

After passing Avranches, the army divided. Part of the force headed west, while the rest swung southeast.

The western force went into Brittany. There, they faced only minimal opposition from the Germans. They occupied most of the region and reached the west coast ports of Brest and Lorient. Their presence distracted the Germans, who started sending troops west to tackle them, only to realize that this was not the main thrust of Patton's advance.

That main thrust was led by the 4th Armored Division and Patton himself. They pushed south and east, crushing German opposition along the way. The enemy was left uncertain about what was happening or how to react. Until they knew where Patton was going, they did not know how to respond. The speed of his advance and the disruption to their communication network made it nearly impossible to work that out.

Assuming that Patton was headed for Paris, the Germans moved troops to counter such an advance. But his intention was different. He was heading southeast, sweeping around the German forces ready to cut them off.

The German Seventh Army, led by General Von Kluge, now lay in the jaws of a trap. Patton's relentless advance had been a massive flanking maneuver that threatened to cut them off from the south.

Hitler, who was 800 miles away in his Wolf's Lair headquarters, finally recognized the difficulty his forces were in. He began giving orders meant to save them from destruction. But so far from the action, he had a poor grasp of what was happening on the ground.

First, he ordered Von Kluge to move four armored divisions from the fight against the British to the American front. But the British had been successful in their aim of thoroughly pinning down the German troops. It took days to disengage from the enemy and extract the Panzers.

Meanwhile, four divisions of the Fifteenth Army were brought around from the Pas de Calais. Hitler had been reluctant to let go of the idea that the Allies were still planning a second invasion there and armored forces had been held in reserve ready to fight that non-existent invasion. But Patton's advance made it clear that the D-Day landings and what followed had been the main event. This was no distraction, no feint, no half of a two-part plan. This was the Western Front, and by holding back resources, Hitler had given the Allies an opportunity to shape it.

Hitler's plan was to launch a counter-attack at Avranches, the site of the gap through which the Americans had emerged. If he could close the gap, then he could isolate Patton, cut off his supply lines, and end his advance.

It was a fine idea in theory but not in reality. The German commanders on the ground advised against such a scheme. They did not have the resources for an effective counterattack against the Allied armies. Allied air power alone would provide a significant hindrance to the scheme.

But Hitler was not to be deterred. Swift, decisive strikes had brought success in the past, beating the numerical odds. They could do it again.

The plan began to fall apart on the way to Avranches. Two infantry and five Panzer divisions ran into an American division at Mortain. Though outnumbered, the Americans fought hard and held their position, delaying the Germans long enough until Allied reinforcements arrived. The Germans were halted.

Hitler was still insistent that Von Kluge should counterattack, but Von Kluge was making other plans. He saw that he could not win where he was and the best long-term hope for Germany lay in preserving the forces he had. He began planning for a withdrawal.

On 8 August, Patton reached Le Mans, far south of the main beachhead. From there, he headed almost directly north, into the rear of Von Kluge's army.

On the same day, the Canadians launched Operation Totalize. In a costly but successful offensive, they punched through the German forces south of Caen and pushed toward the city of Falaise. Like so many offensives, it was not as successful as the commanders hoped, but it threatened to cut the German Seventh Army off from the east.

On the 13th, Patton reached Argentan, not far south of Falaise. On the 14th, the Canadians launched a fresh offensive near the city. Von Kluge's forces were surrounded on every side, with only an 18-mile gap between Patton and the Canadians offering the prospect of retreat to the east.

Von Kluge ordered the retreat, in direct contravention of Hitler's orders. Axis troops began streaming through the Falaise gap.

Inside the isolated pocket of Germans, things looked bad. The French Resistance destroyed some units. Others surrendered to the advancing Allies.

By the 17th of August, the gap was only eleven miles wide. The next day, it was six miles wide, and the Allies were launching relentless air attacks, destroying anyone who tried to escape. On the 21st, American forces in the south met up with Canadian and Polish troops from the north, and the gap was closed.

Von Kluge was relieved of command and recalled to Germany. By now, he had not only disobeyed Hitler's orders, but he had also been implicated in a plot to assassinate the dictator. Rather than face his leader's fury, he committed suicide.

Ten thousand Germans were killed in six days of fighting in the Falaise Pocket. Fifty thousand were taken prisoner. In total, the Germans lost 400,000 men in Normandy, half of whom were taken prisoner. The Allies lost nearly 209,672 men, 36,976 of them were killed.

The remains of the German army were fleeing for the border. Operation Overlord had been a success.

Conclusion

On 19 August, the French Resistance launched a massive uprising in Paris. Terribly weakened by the fighting in Normandy, the Germans were unable to create an effective response. Hitler preferred to see the city burn than allow it to be taken from his grasp, and on the 25th Free French and American forces reached Paris to ensure that did not happen. The capital of France had been liberated, a hugely symbolic moment.

The fighting in France wasn't over, but with the fall of the Falaise Pocket, the outcome was decided. The Allies, now under the overall command of Eisenhower rather than Montgomery, began a great push east. Less than a year after those first brave men leapt off the landing craft in Normandy and waded up the surf into the mouths of German guns, the German empire had fallen. Hitler was dead. His nation was conquered. The atrocities of his regime had been exposed, and the perpetrators sat awaiting trial for their crimes. The D-Day landings played a crucial part in making that happen.

More than 70 years on, it's easy to forget what a staggering and unprecedented achievement D-Day was. It took colossal political, strategic, and logistical efforts to bring together the armed forces of so many countries, to create a plan so daring, and to bring together the resources needed to carry it off.

It also took courage. The men who stepped out onto those beaches knew they were likely walking into a bloodbath. They had trained and prepared for this moment, but it was no less incredible they were willing to put their lives on the line and that, even in the toughest sectors, they made it work. They did not achieve all their objectives because those objectives were ambitious, not because they faltered or failed. Their actions shaped the face of Europe and left an unprecedented mark in the annals of history.

Long may their memory live on.

Can you help me?

If you enjoyed this book, then I'd really appreciate it if you would post a short review on Amazon. I read all the reviews myself so that I can continue to provide books that people want. Thanks for your support!

Preview of Adolf Hitler

A Captivating Guide to the Life of the Führer of Nazi Germany

Introduction

Like someone racing under a snowstorm, tracked by a hunter, Adolf Hitler spent a good part of his life trying to blur the footsteps of his past, but also doing his best to deceive the hunter, stamping new ones. The hunter in this case being the historians who at the emergence of the strong man in Germany—the statesman crushing Europe at lightning speed, plunging the world into the most devastating and costly war ever, and leading to the genocide of Jews, Gypsies and other undesirable groups—began to inquire about the moment and circumstances of his enthronement. How and when was he able to mystify an entire nation? Was he, as Ian Kershaw asked, a natural consequence of German history, or an aberration? Not that Hitler had been in hiding, waiting to attack. The Führer had actually been following an aggressive and savage foreign policy for almost ten years, and been named Man of the Year by *Time* magazine in 1938.

For decades there were uncertainties about his family and childhood; for instance, about the time he was a bohemian vagabond and failed artist in Vienna, about his real achievements as a draftee in World War I, and the details of his rapid rise in the politics of Germany. Everything had been repainted in glorious colors by the Nazi propaganda machine, not to mention that Hitler himself had not given much to talk about in his early days. Some of his most important biographers like Joachim Fest have attributed his obsessive zeal to erase his past to the mind of a skilled propagandist. Today, when Hitler´s zenith has long passed, if there remains a character in history studied to the smallest detail, not only by historians, but also by doctors, psychologists, artists, sociologists, and even architects, it is he. No small irony for someone who went into uncontrollable rage when someone published a photograph of his family or brought to light some unknown aspect of his conflicted and depressive youth.

Like every major leader, Hitler was the product of greater forces than himself, but the Führer knew how to assimilate and throw them against the right target with the promise to give a final solution to the problems of "his" people, adding two essential ingredients to the formula: a mixture of fear and admiration. Thus Hitler was able to drive an enlightened, advanced, and cultured society like Germany into barbarism and genocide. For those who study mass movements, of particular interest is how Hitler, who could not have done anything by himself, could manipulate and submit the will of a whole nation—dismissing the ridiculous notion that he was possessed, or the simplistic explanation that he was crazy. As has been noted on several occasions, if the countless films that show the excitement and hysteria that he aroused in public appearances did not exist, it would be difficult to believe that he had the undeniable support of many Germans and other people.

The psychiatrist Gustav Jung—who once tried to have a respected doctor declare Hitler insane— after seeing him addressing a crowd commented that the Führer, unlike Mussolini whom Jung saw as a mere human, was not "lacking individuality, (he was) confused with his nation's collective soul, and possessed by its Collective Unconscious (...) Not even by the Collective Unconscious of a single nation, but that of an entire race (...) he represents them all, he speaks for all of them. And if he does it shouting, it is because an entire nation, an entire race, is expressing itself through him." On his part, Hitler wrote: "Permanent struggle is the law of life, he who would live must fight." One can assume that he was not thinking uniquely about military matters; his words were influenced by the torturous road that, like many Germans, he had to roam in the difficult first three decades of the twentieth century.

This is not a book about World War II, but about the man, Adolf Hitler, one of the faces and names that still arouse the strongest feelings—repulsion, resentment, and even fanaticism—but one who also had a childhood and a youth, a father and a mother. It is the road to madness—beginning that day in August of 1934 when he took over absolute power and ordered allegiance and loyalty to him alone—that this book is about.

PART I — ORIGINS

"Thus I have drawn the portrait of the young Hitler as well as I can from memory.

But for the question then unknown and expressed which hung above our friendship,

I have not to this day found any answer: What did God want from this person?"

August Kubizek, Hitler's childhood friend, in *The Young Hitler I Knew*

The son of Alois and Klara

One of the biggest challenges any biographer of Adolf Hitler encounters is to reconstruct his early years based on the not-very-abundant sources. Accounts of his youth are almost always filtered through the glass of his later deeds. From the third quarter of the twentieth century, historians began to place greater emphasis on the formative years of great figures—to the extent that they were available—not to psychoanalyze them, but to try to understand the forces that shaped the adults they became. To outline the origins of the Führer requires detective work — objectivity has been obscured, despite the relatively short time passed since his death, not due to lack of sources, but because the historian needs to deal with two equally radical positions: first, those who see in him a budding monster since childhood, evil incarnate, a kind of psychologically and spiritually crippled antichrist, portrayed under the worst possible light; second, the one constituted by a few Nazi sympathizers surviving in the form of revisionism in several volumes of recent apparition, which present him from his early youth as a strong, determined, and brilliant teenager on his way to become one of the greatest leaders of his century, no worse than other statesmen of his time. In this reconstruction one must also deal with the testimony of Hitler himself, and his exaggerated self-glorification in his program and autobiography entitled *Mein Kampf* (My Struggle), written in a Landsberg prison.

The story begins in a very small town of Lower Austria called Strones, now wiped out from the map. Hitler's father, Alois Schicklgruber, was born there. The man with the chubby face and stern expression, whose drooping eyelids he passed onto his son Adolf, came from a family of impoverished peasants that lived between the Danube and the border of Bohemia, among small towns distant from each other, amidst thick forests. The parish archives registered Alois's mother's name, Maria Anna Schicklgruber, but not his father´s. Alois was the natural son of Maria Anna. The identity and ethnicity of Alois's father has been the object of endless speculation, including that he was a Jew and his mother worked as maid for him, but they are nothing more than wild guesses. The identity of his paternal grandfather was already, since Hitler's lifetime, a conundrum that, like other aspects of his family life, was a source of annoyance for the dictator. Maria Schicklgruber later married a miller named Johann Georg Hiedler, when Alois was five. Hiedler may or may not have been Alois's father, but the relationship between Alois and his stepfather must have been cordial, because in adulthood, when he was about forty, Alois officially changed his name to that of his adoptive father, but registering it as "Hitler." It is unclear why he adopted this alternate spelling.

Adolf Hitler's mother was called Klara Pölzl. She was twenty-three years younger than Alois. A soft-looking girl with thick blonde hair, born in Spital, Austria, she was Alois's third wife. There has also been speculation and sensational statements about this woman, such as the well-proven fact that Alois knew her as a maid in his house and made her pregnant when he was still married to his second wife. When he became a widow, he agreed to marry Klara, who was already showing a visible pregnancy. Klara also had blood relation in second degree with Alois, whom she called "Uncle," although they were second cousins. In order to be able to get married, they had to ask for a dispense in the local church. Forty-eight-year-old Alois was an embittered customs officer, strict and inflexible, with an irascible temper and a job that forced him to change his residence with frequency. Based on hard work, he had gone up through the Austrian bureaucracy, not to a privileged economic position but at least to the comfortable middle class. For a time he became a beekeeper and farmer, but that pleasure didn't last.

His wife Klara never got over the initial relationship that had united them, of inferiority and servitude; throughout their life as a couple she remained under him and fulfilled the duties of a servant, attended church, and complied with the orders of the irascible bureaucrat. The union of Alois and Klara produced six children, without much success. The first, Gustav, was born five months after the marriage ceremony, followed by a girl named Ida. Both died of diphtheria a few months apart in the winter of 1888. The conventional assumption is that the third son was Otto, who also died in infancy. Thus the marriage of Alois and Klara was hit by the death of all their children, until their luck changed in 1889 with the birth of Adolf, on April the 20th at 6:30 p.m.

The fourth child was born in a three-story house in Braunau am Inn, now a part of Austria, then a village on the border of the German Empire. Klara, a devout woman, baptized and confirmed their son in the Catholic Church. A fact that has not gone unnoticed by historians and psychiatrists is that during his first five years of life, Adolf was the couple's only child, which earned him special attention both by his mother and father. This does not mean it was precisely beneficial to the child. For his mother, Adolf was, during five crucial years, the son that survived; for his father, the deposit of all his expectations.

Continue reading...

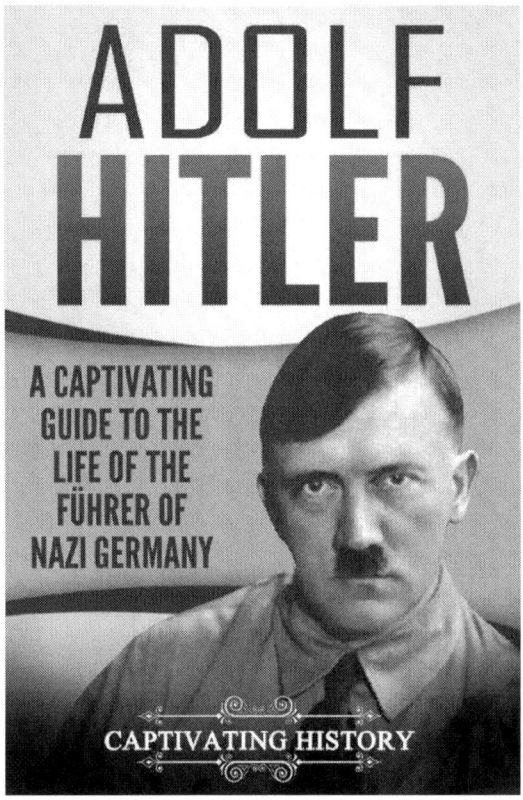

Preview of Winston Churchill:

A Captivating Guide to the Life of Winston S. Churchill

Introduction

As a British politician who was well known for serving twice as prime minister for the United Kingdom and as an infamous war organizer, leader Winston S. Churchill filled his long life with achievements and recognition plotted throughout every modern history book. Most famously, he led Great Britain into victory over Nazi Germany during World War II in his first run as prime minister and played an essential role in negotiating peace once the war reached an unsteady end. Commonly, his name is associated as one of the "Big Three" alongside United States President Franklin D. Roosevelt and Soviet Union leader Joseph Stalin. In unity, the three men helped lead the world to a resolution from the violence and terror that reigned in World War II.

Winston Churchill was more than a military and government leader, though. He lived an entire life full of accomplishments that defined him as a singular person, rather than a government and military leader. In 1953, he won the Nobel Prize for Literature for his "mastery of historical and biographical description as well as for brilliant oratory in defending exalted human values."[i] Although he maintained a somewhat monotone voice over the radio, Churchill excelled in speaking to live crowds as he imparted encouraging words and recounted tales of his life adventures. On top of these accomplishments as a writer and a trailblazer, Churchill is famous for his endless reserves of energy and his need for little sleep, which allowed him to pursue many projects and hobbies outside of his governmental duties.[ii] Among many other possible descriptions, Winton Churchill categorizes as a father, a husband, a painter, a war hero, a politician, a soldier, a smoker, a gambler, and a philosopher.

Any general biography of Winston Churchill will provide an overview of his greatest achievements, but Churchill had other goals and desires that are often ignored and forgotten. What were they? Churchill had a family—a childhood and children of his own—and a political career that began at a young age. He spoke with and entertained some of the biggest names in the world, within both the political and social realms. How did he interact with Franklin D. Roosevelt? With Mahatma Gandhi? Beneath the accolades and accomplishments lies one important question: Who was Winston Churchill out of the spotlight? What were his struggles and personal goals? Was he an average man in some ways? The following book is an outline of Churchill's life that not only gives a brief overview of his best-known feats but also provides a glimpse into who he was as a person.

Chapter One: Churchill's Personal Life

Often, people feel they know much about Winston Churchill as a servant to his country from easily attained and general information, but they know little about Churchill's personal life. Churchill was a husband, a father, a painter, and a historian, among many other things. While he also maintains the status of a war hero and prime minister, he was much more in life. His aspirations and desires were a large part of who he was and how he attained his goals.

An important part of every story lies within the family unit. In 1904, Winston attended a ball in Crewe House—the home of the Earl of Crewe and his wife, Margaret Primrose—where he met Clementine Hozier, the granddaughter of the 10th Earl of Airlie.[iii] In 1908, they found themselves drawn together at another event, hosted by Lady St. Helier. Imaginably, they were instantly compatible because Churchill proposed to Clementine Hozier at Blenheim Palace, his childhood home, later that year, and they married shortly after.[iv]

Over the course of their marriage, Winston and Clementine Churchill had five children: Diana, Randolph, Sarah, Marigold Frances, and Mary. Unfortunately, Marigold grew fatally ill just short of three years after she was born, and the family buried her in the Kensal Green Cemetery.[v] Their other children did not suffer the same fate but provided very interesting personalities and habits which the Churchills had to accommodate on very individual levels. Diana was rather flippant and brought her parents great duress. After two failed marriages and three children, Diana committed suicide in 1963. Randolph, after failing to enter parliament several times, finally found acceptance as a Conservative member of parliament for Preston between 1940 and 1945 and continued to become a successful journalist who began Winston S. Churchill's official biography in the 1960s.[vi] Like his sister, Randolph had two unsuccessful marriages. Additionally, he had two children. Sarah took a career in dramatics, which worked well for a while, but she had the same luck with her love life as her siblings in that she entered two marriages, which ultimately failed, and was then widowed after a third marriage. Mary was the only child who caused her parents little worry or grief. She provided heavy support for them both, especially her mother. Mary's husband, Christopher Soames, was an Assistant Military Attaché in Paris who later found success in parliament. They had five children, and Nicholas, the eldest, was a prominent member of the Conservative Party in his own time.

Although they spent long periods of time apart from one another, Winston and Clementine Churchill maintained a successful marriage, or, rather, as successful as most long marriages prove, generally. As all couples, they had their faults, fights, and failings. In one instance, Clementine hurled a dish of spinach at Churchill, which reportedly missed and splattered behind him. Additionally, she never quite forgave Churchill for buying Chartwell without expressly involving her in the purchase decision, and she brought up her resentment from time to time with a bitter grudge. As stated by Churchill College at Cambridge, "Clementine was high principled and high strung; Winston was stubborn and ambitious," a volatile combination of personality traits within a married couple.[vii]

Churchill spent a good portion of time away from his family, both on business and on holiday. It was a well-known fact that Winston Churchill put work first, but he was devoted to his children, regardless, although he enjoyed spending time abroad with friends and acquaintances much more than his wife and left his children at home; Clementine Churchill often "found the company tedious" and refused to accompany him.[viii] Occasionally, the family would take holidays together, but more often than not, they began taking vacations apart. Churchill holidayed with regularity, visiting wealthy friends in the Mediterranean and cruising with Aristotle Onassis, Greek millionaire ship-owner.[ix] In all, they took eight cruises together. Once when they passed through the Dardanelles, Onassis instructed his crew to pass quietly and during the night so as to avoid drudging up Churchill's bad members of the location.

Winston Churchill's close friends included Professor Lindemann, along with Birkenhead, Beaverbrook, and Bracke—cheerfully dubbed "the three Bs"—of whom Clementine Churchill was never particularly fond. Although Clementine did not often travel with Churchill, the two entertained often as a couple, and their guests included the likes of Charlie Chaplin, Albert Einstein, and Lawrence of Arabia.

In addition to entertaining both his friends and family members, Winston Churchill engaged quite a few personal hobbies. As an amateur artist, Churchill enjoyed painting and employed a special gusto after resigning in 1915 as First Lord of the Admiralty.[x] Paul Maze, a friend of Churchill's whom he met in World War I, taught him to paint early during Churchill's career while providing both companionship and influence. Throughout his painting career, Churchill's skills grew stronger. Churchill is particularly known for his impressionist landscape paintings, and he composed many of these works of art while on holiday in Egypt, Morocco, or the South of France. Not wanting to paint under his own title, Churchill utilized the name "Charles Morin" as a pseudonym and reached the point where he rarely left his home without his painting supplies. Any time he traveled, he tried to slip away for a few moments so that he could spend time with his paints and canvas. Even when Churchill was touring France's Maginot Line in 1939, he still managed to paint with his friends near Dreux.[xi]

Painting was only one of many hobbies Winston employed to pass his free time. Maybe unexpectedly, one of Churchill's greatest vices was a slight gambling addiction, and he lost a small fortune when the American stock market crashed in 1929. Although he maintained a famous name and arose from an upper-class family, Churchill did not believe his income supported his established lifestyle, and the 1929 crash didn't help cushion his ever-slimming pockets. Churchill's income while out of office arrived primarily from book sales and opinion pieces; therefore, he wrote often and well. Winston Churchill has a small library under his name, which includes a novel, two biographies, three volumes of memoirs, and several historical works. In 1953, he gained the Nobel Prize for Literature, and two of his most famous works brought international fame: The Second World War, his six-volume memoir, and *A History of the English-Speaking Peoples*, a four-volume history covering the period from Caesar's invasions of Britain to the beginning of World War I. Additionally, many of Churchill's speeches are in print, such as *Into Battle,* published in the United States under *Blood, Sweat, and Tears,* which *Life Magazine* included as one of the 100 most astounding books published between 1924 and 1944.[xii]

In his spare time at home, Churchill also constructed buildings and garden walls at his house in Chartwell. A few major works he undertook at the country home were building a dam, a swimming pool, and a red brick wall to surround the vegetable garden, as well as retiling a cottage at the end of his garden. In addition to these home improvements, Churchill bought an adjoining farm in 1946 and took up farming.[xiii] On the side, he also bred butterflies, an interest left over from his time in India.[xiv] Moreover, Churchill found great interest in science and technology, delving into a stint of writing popular-science essays on evolution and fusion power. In *Are We Alone in the Universe?*, a mostly forgotten piece of writing, Churchill investigated in an unpublished manuscript the possibility of extraterrestrial life.

To top it all off, Churchill began dabbling in horse-racing in 1949 and took advice from his son-in-law, Christopher Soames, on his first purchase, a three-year-old gray colt named Colonist II, the first of many thoroughbreds. In 1950, Churchill was initiated into the Jockey Club, which much pleased him.[xv]

All in all, Winston S. Churchill had a personal life full of odds-and-ends hobbies, similar to that of any common person. Historians pay close attention to his feats and follies, hoping to gain more insight into the mind of Winston Churchill, the fascinating man who left his mark on history in a way unlike any other. Churchill was a normal man, too, though. He cared for his family, enjoyed the small things in life, and felt that his efforts could be used in many ways.

Continue reading!

Preview of Franklin Roosevelt:

A Captivating Guide to the Life of FDR

Introduction

As the thirty-second president of the United States of America, Franklin Delano Roosevelt (30 January 1882—12 April 1945) is a common household name in both his home country and the world. Known as the man who led the United States through the Great Depression and World War II, Roosevelt was a leader and a statesman, a scholar and a politician. Beginning in 1933, he served as president until his death in 1945, and the general public knows much about this time in his life, with the exception of his poor health, of course, which he kept carefully hidden. Franklin D. Roosevelt is the only president to have served for three consecutive terms, and voted in for a fourth, a fact that allows him to stand out among the long list of American presidents. Notable events during his presidency include the end of the banking crisis; the enacting of the Federal Housing Administration, the Federal Communications Commission, and the Social Security Act; the long epidemic that was World War II; Roosevelt's "Four Freedoms" speech; the Lend-Lease Act with the United Kingdom and the Soviet Union; and the Yalta Conference, among many others.[xvi]

Outside of his role as president of the United States, Franklin D. Roosevelt lived a full life. He was a father and a son, a husband and a career man. He was a bank officer and attended prestigious universities—Harvard University and Columbia University Law School—before practicing law. Additionally, he served as vice president for the Fidelity and Deposit Company. Perhaps most famously, Roosevelt served as governor of New York and president of the United States while he suffered from polio. Instead of allowing the disease to keep him from living a full life, he went above and beyond, training himself to walk without the power of his legs so that his voters would not know that he suffered in any capacity. What this book aims to do is determine who Franklin D. Roosevelt was as a person outside of the spotlight. This book wants to answer questions about this man.

How did he interact with his wife and family? What were his exploits and his vices? His favored hobbies?

The following is an outline of Franklin D. Roosevelt's life that not only gives a brief overview of his best-known feats but also provides a glimpse into who he was as a person. In his inaugural address, Roosevelt said, "This nation asks for action, and action now," and he delivered until his last written words: "The only limit to our realization of tomorrow will be our doubts of today. Let us move forward with strong and active faith."

Chapter One: Childhood and Education

On January 30, 1882, Franklin Delano Roosevelt, named for his mother's uncle Franklin Hughes Delano, [xvii] was born the only child of James Roosevelt and Sara Ann Delano in the Hudson Valley of Hyde Park, New York, at the Roosevelt estate that overlooked the Hudson River, seventy-five miles north of New York City. When his son was born, James Roosevelt wrote in Sara's diary: "At quarter to nine my Sallie had a splendid large boy, but was unconscious when he was born. Baby weighs ten pounds without clothes."[xviii] For a moment, the family was in a tight spot. The mother and child came very close to dying, as the doctor administered too much chloroform due to Sara's intense labor pains. Franklin was not breathing at birth.

Soon overcoming the birth issues, Roosevelt grew up healthily in a privileged family. The estate had been in the family's possession for one hundred years. Both his parents derived from very wealthy and old New York families of English descent. American businessman and horse-breeder, James Roosevelt I worked primarily in the coal and transportation businesses, and he served as vice president for the Delaware and Hudson Railway and also served as president for the Southern Railway Security Company. As the inheritor of a good bit of wealth and a man who held a distaste for the business world, he retired early to the family estate and focused on his health, which was not always well. His family was Dutch, first appearing in America in 1654. Sara Ann Delano was James Roosevelt's second wife, and she devoted her life to caring for her son. Her family was Flemish and arrived in Massachusetts earlier than the Roosevelts appeared in New York. Their families had close ties over the years. Franklin D. Roosevelt's parents were related long distance as sixth cousins.[xix]

At the Roosevelt estate, Franklin spend most of his time with his mother; he grew up in a very patriarchal household. Sara was very protective of her son, while James was relatively absent, although biographer James MacGregor Burns notes that he was more involved than many of his fellow fathers.[xx] Regardless, Roosevelt's mother remained his primary caretaker and influencer for his formative years, neglecting other life and wife duties. Over the years, she formed what some may consider an unhealthy relationship with her son and grew jealous of anyone who held his attention. First and foremost, she wanted to be the most important person in his life and shunned away others, including family. Sara is cited as saying, "My son Franklin is a Delano, not a Roosevelt at all."[xxi]

As many of his status, Franklin did not lack the benefits of his family's privilege. As a five-year-old, Roosevelt visited the White House with his father where President Grover Cleveland told him, "I have one wish for you, little man, that you will never be president of the United States." Little did President Cleveland know that Franklin would hold the record for the most terms in office. In the summers, Roosevelt and his mother spent their days in Fairhaven, Massachusetts, at the Delano Homestead, and every year, Roosevelt's family would travel to Europe where he grew fluent in German and French and the family toured churches, museums, and palaces.[xxii],[xxiii] During this time, Roosevelt began formulating opinions on other countries and their people. Franklin loved France, along with the people who lived there. On the other hand, he claimed that Germany and its citizens were rude and that they constantly said they were better than everyone else. There is a possibility that he inherited his opinions on Germany from his parents who thought that the people were "filthy ... German swine."[xxiv]

During his formative years, Roosevelt dabbled in many sports and hobbies. He learned to shoot, row, ride horses, and play lawn tennis and polo. In his teenage years, he took up golf and learned to sail.[xxv] As befitting the son of a wealthy household, Roosevelt received a sailboat named *New Moon* from his father when he turned sixteen.[xxvi] In his early childhood, Roosevelt received his education at home from private tutors. During this time, he learned varying amounts of French, German, and Spanish, as this was the time that his family traveled often.

Many young men began their boarding schools at twelve, but that idea made Sara incredibly nervous. When he reached the age that his mother considered appropriate, which was fourteen years old, Franklin enrolled in an Episcopal boarding school, Groton School, in Groton, Massachusetts, known as the "bastion of the elite," and he learned alongside students from many other wealthy families.[xxvii] In fact, ninety percent of the attendees were on the social register, a United States document, now outdated, that provides a directory of prominent American families. The document includes members of the social elite who lived within the boundaries of the American upper class, those of "old money" who identify as White Anglo-Saxon Protestants (WASPs).

Here at Groton, Franklin formed a bond with Endicott Peabody, the headmaster who encouraged Christians to engage public service and provide assistance to those less fortunate than them. He said, "If some Groton boys do not enter political life and do something for our land, it won't be because they have not been urged."[xxviii] Peabody was a champion of independent thought, stating that he held no opinions but instead upheld his beliefs, which he claimed were always true and beyond question.[xxix] Of Peabody, Roosevelt later said, "It was a blessing in my life to have the privilege of [his] guiding hand."[xxx] He went as far as to write Peabody a letter after gaining presidency, saying, "For all that you have been and are to me I owe a debt of gratitude."[xxxi] Peabody remained in Franklin's life, serving as the officiate at his wedding and paying a visit to Roosevelt during his presidency.[xxxii]

Although he formed a great bond with the headmaster, Franklin gained little attention while in school. The other students thought he was showy, too eager to gain teachers' attentions. In an attempt to fit in, Franklin purposely garnered demerits in the classroom for small offenses, such as whispering during class time.[xxxiii] His best work was elsewhere, though. While Franklin did not excel in baseball, he stood out as an excellent manager, which helped his leadership skills flourish. In addition, he was a good orator, which allowed him to go far in the debating society. Peabody claimed that Roosevelt was "a quiet, satisfactory boy of more than ordinary intelligence, taking a good position in his form but not brilliant."[xxxiv] Recalling little about him that stood out, another classmate said he was "nice, but completely colorless."[xxxv] What others did notice was that Roosevelt was the only student who self-identified as a Democrat, which followed a family tradition.

Along with many of his classmates, Franklin began Harvard College in 1900 in Cambridge, Massachusetts, [xxxvi] where he joined the Alpha Delta Phi fraternity[xxxvii] and the Fly Club,[xxxviii] along with the Signet Society and the Hasty Pudding Club. He majored in history and political science while in college but showed no express interest in college work itself, and often cut classes. In fact, he escaped out a window during one lecture and climbed down a fire escape while the professor had his attention elsewhere. Therefore, he kept a "gentleman's C" in most classes, which means that he barely managed to pass. Just as at Groton, Roosevelt's classmates at Harvard held various opinions on him. One of his cousins, Alice, said, "He was a good little mother's boy whose friends were dull, who belonged to the minor clubs, and who never was at the really gay parties."[xxxix] In light of such, Franklin had to earn his name elsewhere.

Roosevelt gained the titles of president and editor of *The Harvard Crimson*, Harvard's daily newspaper, during his last year. In this position, he learned leadership and responsibility while developing a taste for ambition. The staff members said that he was "a king of frictionless command," a trait that followed Roosevelt throughout the rest of his life.[xl]

Looking back on his classes, Roosevelt said, "I took economics courses in college for four years, and everything I was taught was wrong."[xli] He graduated in 1903 with a Bachelor of Arts degree in history. In 1904, Roosevelt gained entry into Columbia Law School but decided to quit in 1907 after he passed the New York State Bar exam. In 1929, Franklin received an honorary LL.D. from Harvard,[xlii] and he received a posthumous J.D. from Columbia Law School.[xliii]

Continue reading!

Check out more books by Captivating History

If you're interested in mythology, check out books by Matt Clayton

Free Bonus from Captivating History (Available for a Limited time)

Hi History Lovers!

Now you have a chance to join our exclusive history list so you can get your first history ebook for free as well as discounts and a potential to get more history books for free! Simply visit the link below to join.

Captivatinghistory.com/ebook

Also, make sure to follow us on:

Twitter: @Captivhistory

Facebook: Captivating History: @captivatinghistory

Bibliography

Hugh Ambrose (2010), *The Pacific.*

Jim Baggott (2009), *Atomic: The First War of Physics and the Secret History of the Atom Bomb, 1939-49.*

Ralph Bennett (1999), *Behind the Battle: Intelligence in the War with Germany 1939-1945.*

Nigel Cawthorne (2004), *Turning the Tide: Decisive Battles of the Second World War.*

Francis Crosby (2010), *The Complete Guide to Fighters & Bombers of the World.*

John Ellis (1993), *The World War II Databook.*

Ian V. Hogg and John Weeks (1980), *The Illustrated Encyclopedia of Military Vehicles.*

Richard Holmes, ed. (2001), *The Oxford Companion to Military History.*

John Keegan (1987), *The Mask of Command.*

Orr Kelly (2002), *Meeting the Fox: The Allied Invasion of Africa, from Operation Torch to Kasserine Pass to Victory in Tunisia.*

James Lucas (1986), *Last Days of the Reich.*

James Lucas (1996), *Hitler's Enforcers: Leaders of the German War Machine 1939-1945.*

David Rooney (1999), *Military Mavericks: Extraordinary Men of Battle.*

Conrad Totman (2005), *A History of Japan*, second edition.

Charles Whiting (1999), *West Wall: The Battle for Hitler's Siegfried Line.*

---

[i] "The Nobel Prize in Literature 1953." *The Official Website of the Nobel Prize.* http://www.nobelprize.org/nobel_prizes/literature/laureates/1953/. Accessed 18 May 2017.

[ii] "Sir Winston Churchill: A Chronology." *Churchill College, Cambridge.* https://www.chu.cam.ac.uk/archives/collections/churchill-papers/churchill-biography/. Accessed 22 May 2017.

[iii] "Sir Winston Churchill: A Chronology." *Churchill College, Cambridge.* https://www.chu.cam.ac.uk/archives/collections/churchill-papers/churchill-biography/. Accessed 22 May 2017.

[iv] Soames, Mary. *Speaking for Themselves: The Private Letters of Sir Winston and Lady Churchill.* 1999.

[v] Soames, Mary. *Speaking for Themselves: The Private Letters of Sir Winston and Lady Churchill.* 1999.

[vi] "Sir Winston Churchill: A Chronology." *Churchill College, Cambridge.* https://www.chu.cam.ac.uk/archives/collections/churchill-papers/churchill-biography/. Accessed 22 May 2017.

[vii] "Sir Winston Churchill: A Chronology." *Churchill College, Cambridge.* https://www.chu.cam.ac.uk/archives/collections/churchill-papers/churchill-biography/. Accessed 22 May 2017.

[viii] Soames, Mary. *Speaking for Themselves: The Private Letters of Sir Winston and Lady Churchill.* 1999.

[ix] "Sir Winston Churchill: A Chronology." *Churchill College, Cambridge.* https://www.chu.cam.ac.uk/archives/collections/churchill-papers/churchill-biography/. Accessed 22 May 2017.

[x] Jenkins, Roy. *Churchill: A Biography.* 2011.

[xi] "Sir Winston Churchill: A Chronology." *Churchill College, Cambridge.* https://www.chu.cam.ac.uk/archives/collections/churchill-papers/churchill-biography/. Accessed 22 May 2017.

[xii] Canby, Henry Seidel, and editors. "The 100 Outstanding Books of 1924-1944." *Life.* August 1944.

[xiii] "Sir Winston Churchill: A Chronology." *Churchill College, Cambridge.* https://www.chu.cam.ac.uk/archives/collections/churchill-papers/churchill-biography/. Accessed 22 May 2017.

[xiv] Wainright, Martin. "Winston Churchill's Butterfly House Brought Back to Life." *The Guardian.* August 2010. https://www.theguardian.com/environment/2010/aug/19/winston-churchill-butterfly. Accessed 22 May 2017.

[xv] "Sir Winston Churchill: A Chronology." *Churchill College, Cambridge.* https://www.chu.cam.ac.uk/archives/collections/churchill-papers/churchill-biography/. Accessed 22 May 2017.

[xvi] Abate, Frank R. *The Oxford Desk Dictionary of People and Places.* 1999. https://books.google.com/books?id=6xxYAgAAQBAJ&pg=PA329#v=onepage&q&f=false. Accessed 20 June 2017.

[xvii] "Roosevelt's Genealogy." *Franklin D. Roosevelt Presidential Library and Museum.* http://www.fdrlibrary.marist.edu/archives/resources/genealogy.html. Accessed 19 June 2017.

[xviii] Marrin, Albert. *FDR and the American Crisis.* 2015.

[xix] Burns, James MacGregor. *Roosevelt.* 1956.

[xx] Burns, James MacGregor. *Roosevelt.* 1956.

[xxi] Burns, James MacGregor. *Roosevelt.* 1956.

[xxii] Smith, Jean Edward. *FDR*. 2007.

[xxiii] Marrin, Albert. *FDR and the American Crisis*. 2015.

[xxiv] Marrin, Albert. *FDR and the American Crisis*. 2015.

[xxv] Smith, Jean Edward. *FDR*. 2007.

[xxvi] Black, Conrad. *Franklin Delano Roosevelt: Champion of Freedom*. 2005.

[xxvii] Marrin, Albert. *FDR and the American Crisis*. 2015.

[xxviii] Marrin, Albert. *FDR and the American Crisis*. 2015.

[xxix] Marrin, Albert. *FDR and the American Crisis*. 2015.

[xxx] Burns, James MacGregor. *Roosevelt*. 1956.

[xxxi] Marrin, Albert. *FDR and the American Crisis*. 2015.

[xxxii] Gunther, John. *Roosevelt in Retrospect*. 1950.

[xxxiii] Marrin, Albert. *FDR and the American Crisis*. 2015.

[xxxiv] Smith, Jean Edward. *FDR*. 2007.

[xxxv] Gunther, John. *Roosevelt in Retrospect*. 1950.

[xxxvi] Gunther, John. *Roosevelt in Retrospect*. 1950.

[xxxvii] "Family of Wealth Gave Advantages." *New York Times*. 13 April 1945. http://www.nytimes.com/learning/general/onthisday/bday/0130.html. Accessed 20 June 2017.

[xxxviii] Gunther, John. *Roosevelt in Retrospect*. 1950.

[xxxix] Marrin, Albert. *FDR and the American Crisis*. 2015.

[xl] Marrin, Albert. *FDR and the American Crisis*. 2015.

[xli] Burns, James MacGregor. *Roosevelt*. 1956.

[xlii] "Obama Joins List of Seven Presidents with Harvard Degrees." *Harvard Gazette*. 6 November 2008. http://news.harvard.edu/gazette/story/2008/11/obama-joins-list-of-seven-presidents-with-harvard-degrees/. Accessed 20 June 2017.

xliii Kelly, Erin. "Presidents Roosevelt Awarded Posthumous J.D.s." *Columbia Law School.* 25 September 2008.
http://www.law.columbia.edu/media_inquiries/news_events/2008/september2008/ roosevelt_jds. Accessed 20 June 2017.

21725779R00132

Printed in Poland
by Amazon Fulfillment
Poland Sp. z o.o., Wrocław